The Press:
Free and Responsible?

EDITED BY Hoyt H. Purvis

Lyndon B. Johnson School of Public Affairs

Lyndon Baines Johnson Library

Symposia Series

1982

ISBN: 0-89940-411-1
Library of Congress Catalog Card Number: 82-81870
Copyright *1982* by the Board of Regents, The University of Texas
All rights reserved
Printed in the United States of America
Cover and book designed by WHITEHEAD & WHITEHEAD, AUSTIN, TEXAS

Contents

Preface v
Participants vii
Introduction HOYT PURVIS 1

I. Can the First Amendment Survive a Free Press? 15
    Opening Remarks by JOHN B. CONNALLY 15
    Panel Statements 24
        ARTHUR GINSBURG, *Moderator* 24
        EDWARD L. BARRETT, JR. 27
        DOUGLASS CATER 29
        ARCHIBALD COX 30
        THOMAS GEE 31
        JOSEPH KRAFT 32
        MARIANNE MEANS 34
        HARRISON E. SALISBURY 36
        KENNETH TOWERY 38
    Panel Discussion 38

II. How Responsible Can a Free, Competitive Press Be? 63
    Opening Remarks by JODY POWELL 63
    Panel Statements 66
        DWIGHT TEETER, *Moderator* 66
        PETER BRAESTRUP 67
        HODDING CARTER III 70
        GEORGE CHRISTIAN 72
        ANTHONY DAY 73
        MARK MCKINNON 75
        HERBERT SCHMERTZ 77
        DANIEL SCHORR 80
        JODY POWELL 82
    Panel Discussion 83
    Concluding Remarks by JIM LEHRER 98

Preface

This volume resulted from a symposium cosponsored by the Lyndon Baines Johnson Library and The University of Texas at Austin on April 3, 1981 in the LBJ Auditorium on the Austin campus.

This was the fifteenth national symposium held at the LBJ Library, a series initiated by President Lyndon Johnson soon after the Library was dedicated in 1971.

The symposia have covered a wide range of important topics relating to government, society, and public policy. The subject of this symposium—press freedom and responsibility—was particularly relevant and stimulating, considering the pervasive nature and key role of the media in American society and public affairs.

In addition to those who participated in the deliberations, those taking part in the symposium program included William S. Livingston, Vice President and Dean of Graduate Studies, The University of Texas at Austin; Edward Weldon, Deputy Archivist of the United States; J.J. (Jake) Pickle, United States Representative, Tenth District, Texas; Harry J. Middleton, Director, Lyndon Baines Johnson Library; and Elspeth Rostow, Dean, Lyndon B. Johnson School of Public Affairs, The University of Texas at Austin.

There were two symposium sessions. Part I was entitled "Can the First Amendment Survive a Free Press?," and was preceded by an address by John Connally, former Texas Governor and Cabinet member. Part II, "How Responsible Can a Free, Competitive Press Be?" was opened with an address by Jody Powell, Press Secretary to President Jimmy Carter.

For purposes of clarification and to provide readers with background information on some of the specific individuals and issues mentioned in the symposium discussion—particularly legal actions and court cases—a number of editor's notes have been included.

Participants

EDWARD L. BARRETT, JR. is Professor and Dean of the School of Law at the University of California at Davis. He has also served as a law professor at the University of California School of Law at Berkeley. His professional interests have centered around the criminal justice system and its reform, criminal law and procedure, the administration of criminal justice, and constitutional law, for which he has written a case book. He has written on a number of First Amendment issues.

PETER BRAESTRUP is Editor of the *Wilson Quarterly*, published by the Woodrow Wilson International Center for Scholars in Washington, D.C. Braestrup has worked for the *New York Herald-Tribune, New York Times*, and *Washington Post*, and was a Nieman Fellow at Harvard. His two-volume *Big Story: How the American Press and Television Reported and Interpreted the Tet Crisis* won the 1978 Sigma Delta Chi Award.

HODDING CARTER III served as Assistant Secretary of State for Public Affairs and as Chief Spokesman for the State Department during the Carter Administration. He was editor of the *Delta Democrat-Times* in Greenville, Mississippi, and was a Nieman Fellow at Harvard. He has also been the anchorman for "Inside Story," a public television series examining press performance.

DOUGLASS CATER is now Trustee, Senior Fellow, and Member of the Program Council of the Aspen Institute for Humanistic Studies. He has been Vice-Chairman of the London *Observer* and President of Observer International. Earlier he was Washington Editor of *Reporter* magazine and a Special Assistant to President Johnson. He is the author of *The Fourth Branch of Government*, an examination of the role of the press in Washington, and has written on a number of issues involving the role of communications in society.

GEORGE CHRISTIAN was Press Secretary to President Lyndon Johnson and earlier served as Press Secretary to Texas Governor John Connally and as Executive Assistant to Governor Price Daniel. Early in his career he worked as a wire-service reporter. He is the author of *The President Steps Down* and is now president of an Austin-based media relations firm.

JOHN B. CONNALLY, JR. is now a partner in the Houston law firm of Vinson and Elkins. He began his lengthy career of public service as Administrative Assistant to Senator Lyndon Johnson, and later served as Secretary of the Navy, Governor of Texas (1963-69), and Secretary of the Treasury. He was an unsuccessful Republican presidential aspirant in 1980. He serves on the boards of a number of corporations and institutions.

ARCHIBALD COX is Carl M. Loeb University Professor at the Harvard Law School. He was first appointed to the Harvard law faculty in 1946, and has held distinguished law chairs between periods of government service. He has been Chairman of the Wage Stabilization Board, Solicitor for the Department of Labor, and Solicitor General of the United States. He was the Watergate special prosecutor from May 1973 until he was dismissed in October 1973 in the infamous "Saturday Night Massacre." He has authored a number of books, and is Chairman of the governing board of Common Cause.

ANTHONY DAY is Editor of the editorial pages of the *Los Angeles Times*. A graduate of Harvard, he was also a Nieman Fellow. He was a reporter with the Philadelphia *Bulletin* and worked for nine years in the *Bulletin*'s Washington bureau. He is a member of the board of directors of the American Society of Newspaper Editors, and has served as Chairman of the Freedom of Information Committee of ASNE.

THOMAS GIBBS GEE was educated at the Citadel, the United States Military Academy, and The University of Texas Law School. He practiced law first in Houston, and from 1954 to 1973 in Austin. In August 1973, he was appointed Judge of the United States Court of Appeals for the Fifth Circuit.

ARTHUR L. GINSBURG is a Visiting Professor in the Department of Journalism of The University of Texas at Austin. Ginsburg, who has a law degree from Temple University, previously served as Chief of the Complaints and Compliance Division of the Federal Communications Commission.

JOSEPH KRAFT is a syndicated columnist. Educated at Columbia and Princeton, he worked for the *Washington Post* as an editorial writer, for the *New York Times*, and for *Harper's* magazine as Washington correspondent. He served as a speech writer for John Kennedy in 1960, and has written for most of the major magazines in the country. He has authored a number of books and is the recipient of numerous awards.

JIM LEHRER is anchorman and Associate Editor of the Mac-Neil-Lehrer Report on public television. Lehrer has won a number of awards, including the George Polk Award and the Peabody Award, for his television work. He is a graduate of the University of Missouri, and wrote for the *Dallas Times-Herald* and *Dallas Morning News* before beginning his television career with KERA in Dallas.

MARK MCKINNON was Editor of the *Daily Texan*, the University of Texas at Austin student newspaper, in 1980-81. During his tenure as *Texan* editor, McKinnon was arrested, fined, and jailed briefly on a charge of contempt of court for refusing to comply with a request to turn over unpublished editorial material. McKinnon has also worked as a songwriter.

MARIANNE MEANS writes a syndicated column for King Features Syndicate. She has covered Washington politics and national events for eighteen years. She has also been Washington correspondent and White House correspondent for the Hearst Newspapers. Means has authored a number of books and articles and has been a frequent radio commentator and television panelist. She has a degree from the George Washington University Law Center.

JODY POWELL was Press Secretary to Jimmy Carter when he was Governor of Georgia and during the 1976 Presidential campaign. Powell then became White House Press Secretary during the Carter Presidency. He is writing a book about the White House and the press.

HARRISON E. SALISBURY began his journalistic career with the United Press. He then served as Assistant Managing Editor, Associate Editor, and Editor of the "Op-Ed" page of the *New York Times*. He was also that newspaper's Moscow correspondent, and is a specialist in Soviet and communist affairs. Salisbury has won the Pulitzer Prize and numerous other journalistic awards. He has also been a television commentator, and is the author of many books, including several on Russia. His most recent book is *Without Fear or Favor*, a study of the *New York Times*.

HERBERT SCHMERTZ is Director and Vice-President of Mobil Oil Corporation. A lawyer, he was General Counsel and Assistant to the Director of the Federal Mediation and Conciliation Service before joining Mobil in 1966. At Mobil his portfolio includes public affairs, corporate public relations, and domestic and international relations, and he has been associated with Mobil's public affairs advertising campaign. In 1980 he worked in Senator Edward Kennedy's campaign for the Democratic Presidential nomination.

DANIEL SCHORR is Senior Correspondent for the Cable News Network and for twenty-five years was a national and foreign correspondent for CBS. He resigned from CBS in 1976 following a controversy in which he refused, on First Amendment grounds, to reveal a confidential source to the House Ethics Committee. Schorr has been widely honored for his defense of First Amendment freedoms, as well as for his Watergate coverage and reporting from the Soviet Union. He has been a Regents' Professor of Journalism at the University of California in Berkeley. His experiences are described in his book, *Clearing the Air*.

DWIGHT L. TEETER, JR. is Chairman of the Department of Journalism of The University of Texas at Austin. He has also taught at the University of Kentucky. A graduate of the University of California, Teeter has a Ph.D. from the University of Wisconsin. He has written extensively on mass communications law, and is coauthor of a textbook on the subject.

R. KENNETH TOWERY is a political and business consultant with long experience in both journalism and government. He won the Pulitzer Prize for reporting in 1954 for a series of stories in the Cuero, Texas, *Record* exposing fraud and corruption in the Texas Veterans' Land Program. He was Press Secretary and later Administrative Assistant to Senator John Tower and was Deputy Director of the United States Information Agency.

HOYT PURVIS, editor of this volume, is on the faculty of the Lyndon B. Johnson School of Public Affairs. From 1977 to 1980 he was Foreign/Defense Policy Adviser to Senate Majority Leader Robert Byrd and Deputy Director of the Senate Majority Policy Committee. Earlier he served as Press Secretary and Special Assistant to Senator J. W. Fulbright. Purvis also has extensive experience in communications and publications, and edited *The Presidency and the Press*, published in 1976. He is Chairman of the Austin Cable Television Commission.

Introduction

Freedom of the press is a fundamental American right.
"Responsibility" of the press is a fundamental American issue.
These two principles—freedom and responsibility—often come into conflict, or threaten to do so.
Trying to reconcile them raises a number of important issues, particularly when such legal questions as "fair trial vs. free press," newsman's privilege, and confidentiality of journalistic sources are stirred in, along with broader topics such as media credibility, "manipulation" of the media, and the increasing concentration of media ownership.
Given the pervasive nature of the mass media in today's society, and the influence of the media on politics and public affairs, these questions become all the more important.
These were the issues which were discussed and debated by a distinguished group of journalists, jurists, scholars, and former public officials (including two men who served as Presidential press secretaries) in a symposium cosponsored by the Lyndon Baines Johnson Library and The University of Texas at Austin.

Credibility and Responsibility Questions

The symposium, which was the basis for this book, took place on April 3, 1981. It occurred between two events that raised significant questions about press credibility and responsibility. The first of these, which was referred to several times during the symposium, was the media coverage of the attempted assassination of President Reagan on March 30, 1981. With their compulsion to be "first" with news, the television networks made several inaccurate and misleading reports about developments related to the assassination attempt. The most egregious of these was the report that White House Press Secretary James Brady had died of his wounds.

Only a few weeks after the symposium, there was great

controversy over the Pulitzer Prize awarded to a *Washington Post* reporter for an article entitled "Jimmy's World," a report about an eight-year-old heroin addict. After the prize had been awarded, it was learned that the story had been fabricated. Although admitting that Jimmy did not exist, the reporter insisted he was a "composite" character. The *Post* returned the Pulitzer and editorially apologized for printing the story. The newspaper referred to the article as a "weird and atypical hoax," but it said, "You may be plenty sure that there will be lots of self-examination, that the episode will be written about and explained in this paper and that more of the skepticism and heat that our colleagues traditionally bring to bear on the outside world will now be trained on our own interior workings. One of these episodes is too many."[1]

At the time of its original publication, the article had generated considerable local attention. Local authorities had conducted a search for "Jimmy," but the *Post* had refused to cooperate with them on the grounds that its reporter's life might have been endangered if she had disclosed the true identity of the subject. The reporter said she had obtained the story only on the condition that she would not disclose her sources. The *Post* initially stood by the reporter's right to conceal her sources; indeed, none of the editorial staff pressed the reporter to tell the identity.

The Pulitzer hoax focused attention on the increasing tendency to use unidentified sources and quotes in news stories. As *New York Times* columnist Anthony Lewis wrote, "In recent years the confidential source has become a mythic figure in American journalism."[2] Ironically, it was the *Post* that had given heightened respectability to the use of unidentified sources with its "Deep Throat" source during Watergate. But the *Post* had also made a point of engaging in meticulous double-checking of information in its widely acclaimed Watergate reporting. Such double-checking clearly did not occur in the case of the "Jimmy" story.

The dramatic impact of the Watergate reporting gave rise to a great emphasis on "investigative" reporting. Journalism schools were overrun with students who wanted to be investigative reporters. No doubt spurred by the competi-

---

[1] "The End of the 'Jimmy' Story," editorial, *Washington Post*, April 16, 1981.

[2] Anthony Lewis, "First Amendment Hubris," *New York Times*, April 19, 1981.

tion, publishers and broadcasting executives were pressuring editors for such reporting. In turn, editors pushed reporters to come up with articles about scandals and misdeeds. Meanwhile, some traditional journalistic practices were de-emphasized. The growing reliance on unattributed sources also made it increasingly possible for some public figures and politicians to use the confidentiality shield to leak information favorable to them or unfavorable to their opponents.

The impact of Watergate also helped make journalists into celebrities. If the sources were anonymous, the journalists were certainly not.

The glamorization of journalists was accompanied by some other important journalistic trends. First, there had been what was sometimes called the "new journalism," initially popularized by writers such as Gay Talese and Tom Wolfe. The new journalism employed more of a literary than a reportorial approach. In many cases writers injected a particular point of view in the articles, or took an advocacy approach. This was a far cry from the traditional goal of "objective" journalism. In some cases "constructed" dialogue rather than standard quotations were used. "Composite" characters rather than real people were sometimes utilized to tell a story. It might be said that the "Jimmy" story was a logical if corrupt extension of the new journalism.

The introduction of new journalism was followed by another trend—the emphasis on personalities in media coverage. In 1968, the *Washington Post* introduced its "Style" section, which was widely imitated. There was less attention to routine coverage of events, and more to personalities. A "Style" editor described the approach:

> Style's focus is squarely on the human dimension, a dimension that somehow got cut wafer-thin in the who-what-when-where-why formula that seemed nearly computer-programed by the early '60s....Style writers are striving to gather facts without excising their human context, freeze-drying their emotional impact. They try to make contact with the private individual behind the public image.[3]

---

[3]Thomas R. Kendrick, "Introduction," in *Writing in Style*, ed. Laura Longley Babb (Washington, D.C.: Washington Post Co., 1975), p. iii. (Distributed by Houghton Mifflin, Boston.)

Obviously there are some attractive elements in this approach, and some excellent writing has resulted. But this personality journalism has often spilled over into "serious" news coverage, as opposed to feature articles. Magazine journalism and television have clearly influenced efforts by newspapers to come up with a journalistic formula more appropriate for a multimedia age.

When style prevails over substance, the ramifications can be profound—and not just because this kind of journalism is often more readable, more entertaining, and may sell more newspapers and advertising. It also affects the way readers perceive developments in society. There has been an increasing emphasis on "assessment" journalism as well. This is not the same as advocacy journalism, because the writer is not necessarily advocating a point of view; rather, he is evaluating developments and making judgments. The writer gives his interpretation of what is *really* happening—or who is winning—at least from his perspective.

Television, and its style of coverage, has had considerable influence on the other media. Of course, television excels at live, on-the-spot coverage of major events. But television is geared to action and, preferably, confrontation. The prototypical TV coverage involves a "story line," a dramatic strain that runs through a particular event.

Meanwhile, would-be newsmakers are busy trying to set up "photo opportunities" to grab the attention of the media, with political candidates and their professional campaignocrats often staging events with TV coverage first in their minds. And, as several symposium participants noted, it is frequently easier to get news coverage if a demonstration, a march, or some other visually interesting event is involved.

Television has also contributed to what has been called "ambush" journalism. This stratagem involves trapping an unsuspecting or reluctant interviewee and then bombarding him, on camera, with tough questions. In some cases this has involved cameramen and reporters "staking out" or pursuing a subject down the street—with cameras rolling.

As is true with some of the other modern journalistic techniques, this approach has, in some cases, been effective and appropriate. But these techniques have also been abused and carried to extremes.

Perhaps the Pulitzer hoax served to stimulate some useful self-examination by the media on some of these journalistic practices, and on the broader issues of press freedom and responsibility, which are the subjects of this volume.

Actually there were several other controversies involving major news stories in the same period. The Pulitzer Prize for feature writing, which had originally been awarded to *Post* reporter Janet Cooke, was subsequently given to Teresa Carpenter of the *Village Voice*, and even this award came under fire in some quarters. Carpenter wrote about Dennis Sweeney, the admitted murderer of Allard Lowenstein, former Member of Congress and long-time political activist. Although many readers believed the article strongly implied that Carpenter had interviewed Sweeney, it was learned that she had never talked with him.[4] Others objected to what they considered to be malicious and unfounded charges in the article. The National News Council, an independent body which investigates complaints about inaccuracy or unfairness in news reports—and is itself somewhat controversial—said Carpenter's article was "marred by the over-use of unattributed sources, by a writing style so colored and imaginative as to blur precise meanings, and by such reckless and speculative construction as to result in profound unfairness to the victim of a demented killer."[5] The *Village Voice* defended the story and attacked the Council, which is composed of prominent representatives of the public and press, saying that "it is troublesome that a quasi-official body attempts to police the press."[6]

Another controversy centered around a *New York Daily News* columnist, Michael Daly, for his reporting from Northern Ireland. Daly's account of incidents was challenged by the London *Daily Mail* as "a work of pure imagination."[7] Upon examination, it was learned that many statements in Daly's articles were incorrect. Daly, who resigned as a result of the controversy, acknowledged having used a pseudonym for a soldier who was featured in his

---

[4]The original article appear in the *Village Voice*, May 12, 1980.

[5]"National News Council Report," *Columbia Journalism Review*, 20, no. 3 (September/October 1981): 86.

[6]Ibid.

[7]Mitchell Stephens, "More 'Jimmy' Fallout," *Washington Journalism Review* 3, no. 6 (July/August 1981): 13.

writing, and admitted recreating scenes that he had not witnessed.

Still another flap occurred over a *Washington Post* article recounting the life of John W. Hinckley, Jr., the accused assailant of President Reagan and three others. Hinckley had been a student at Texas Tech in Lubbock, and the *Post* reported, "A penchant for guns hardly strikes anyone as ominous in freewheeling Lubbock, where some university students carry guns to class and the pistol-packing frontier Texas tradition runs deep and long."[8] A *Dallas Times-Herald* columnist wrote, "The *Post*'s portrait of the city and the university was every bit as fictionalized as its story on the mysterious eight-year-old Jimmy...."[9]

Later, the *Post* printed a correction: "Texas Tech students do not carry guns to class...and the city itself is a quiet town with orderly and law-abiding citizens. There is no 'pistol-packing' tradition in Lubbock, as the article incorrectly implied."[10] The *Post* said the inaccuracy resulted from an incorrect interpretation of a report appearing in another newspaper.

These examples must be seen against a broader background of strong performances by many elements of the American media, and numerous cases of solid and successful investigative reporting. But these episodes served to raise questions about media credibility and responsibility, as did such occurrences as network television interviews with convicted killers Sirhan Sirhan and Charles Manson.

As *Newsweek* commented, "There is nothing more important to journalists and journalism than credibility—and even before 'Jimmy's World' was exposed as a hoax, the public had reservations about how much the news media could be trusted."[11]

Confidence in the Media

Public confidence in the media was a topic which frequently came up at the symposium. In his remarks opening the symposium, John Connally flatly asserted that the public has lost confidence in the press.

---

[8]*Washington Post*, April 5, 1981.

[9]Bronson Havard, "Texas Tech and the Post," *Dallas Times-Herald*, April 10, 1981.

[10]*Washington Post*, April 30, 1981.

[11]"A Searching of Conscience," *Newsweek* 97, no. 18 (May 4, 1981): 50.

According to a Louis Harris study, confidence in the press has declined rather steadily over a fifteen-year period, although it leveled off some in the last five years. The percentage of people expressing "a great deal of confidence" in the press in November 1980 was 19 percent, a net loss of 10 percent since 1966. According to Harris, confidence in TV news has been consistently higher than in newspapers, but it too has shown a net loss in public confidence.[12]

A *Newsweek* poll taken in April 1981 reported that fully a third of those who knew about the Pulitzer scandal rejected the view that it was an isolated incident, believing instead that reporters often make things up. Most of those interviewed gave television news programs, news magazines, and daily newspapers relatively high marks for accuracy and lack of bias, but more than 60 percent said they believed "only some" or "very little" of what they read in the press or heard on television.[13]

According to Connally, a major reason for this "loss of confidence" is that "the press all too frequently says that good news is no news; only bad news is news." (Ironically, in making this familiar assertion against the press, Connally was echoing a charge frequently made by Third World countries against the Western press—that it prints only "bad" news about their countries, and very little that is good or positive. When the charge is made about the Western press, many public and media figures in the U.S.—perhaps a little too self-righteously—immediately start declaiming about freedom of the press and efforts by Third World countries to "manage" the news. And, indeed, some in the Third World have made attempts to restrict press coverage.)

Connally's salvos against the media were met with a return of fire from several sides. His comments provided an ample agenda for the assembled panelists to discuss.

Connally said, "We will continue to have a free press so long as we have a responsible press. But a responsible press cannot be negative in its character. A responsible press, in my judgment, cannot long take the attitude...that the only news is bad news."

Television newsman Daniel Schorr, while taking a

---

[12]Louis Harris Surveys, *Washington Journalism Review* 3, no. 3 (April 1981): 22.

[13]"A Newsweek Poll: How the News Media Rate," poll conducted by the Gallup Organization, *Newsweek* 97, no. 18 (May 4, 1981): 51.

sharply differing view from Connally, nonetheless said, "It is idle to overlook the fact that there is suspicion, reservation, worry, concern, and hostility among people in America today" about the media....People feel they are being force-fed, that they are being given diets of violence and sex for ratings points and millions of dollars, that the news is somehow manipulated."

Several participants pointed to the special role that the press plays in American society, and its responsibility to publish all the news—good and bad. Harrison Salisbury, long-time correspondent for the *New York Times*, recalled his experience as a Moscow correspondent: "I lived and worked for many years in a country where the press published only good news, no bad news....It published no negative news, particularly about the government. There was no sensationalism in this press, very dull headlines...."

Anthony Day, editor of the *Los Angeles Times* editorial pages, offered another perspective and one that bears remembering. He maintained that sometimes the press, "in order to fill its obligations to itself and its readers, has to run the risk of appearing to be absolutely irresponsible." Day said, "Being responsible too often means following conventional wisdom or prevailing opinion or listening to strong and powerful government claims." He added, "What is commonly thought to be responsible is not always responsible."

Former Presidential Press Secretary George Christian noted that "the press is the only one of our great national institutions with an objective which is essentially negative. The press focuses on blemishes and imperfections. By its nature, it is constantly picking over old bones, looking for mistakes. So it fulfills a useful, if sometimes morbid, purpose in our society."

But, as syndicated columnist Marianne Means said,

> the reason that we like bad news, if you want to put it that way, is that it is the nature of the business. The unique events, the dramatic events—that is what, frankly, sells papers. The public is curious. It wants to know about unusual things that are going on. We are in the business of informing, and not all of us like to admit it, but we are also in the business of entertaining. Also, we don't invent these things, we merely report them.

Media Economics

These "economic" issues frequently came up in the discussion. Not the media coverage of economic issues—Connally's point about the weakness of economic reporting and analysis was hard to argue with. Rather, the issue was the "economics" of the media, the business side.

But here there seemed to be some contradictions, or at least a paradox. Connally extolled the virtues of the free-enterprise system, and insisted that the media should be more supportive of the U.S. economic system: "Most of those in the press take the position that it is not their responsibility to defend this economic system. Then whose is it? They exist because of it. They prosper because of this economic system."

The fact is that the media are very much part of that economic system and it is the profit motive that often engenders the kind of coverage that Connally and others deplore. As Marianne Means commented, "it is the nature of the business."

The media are in business. The vast majority of publishers and broadcasters design their papers, magazines, and programming to sell—either to a specific audience, or, more often, to a broad audience. And they are generally going to sell to the public what it wants to buy. Regrettably, the public does not necessarily want, for example, to read an analysis of supply-side economics. There may be more interest in reading about the Son of Sam murders. Some of us might like to see more of what author Stephen Hess has called "social science journalism." But, as Hess writes in his book, *The Washington Reporters*,

> Social science journalism may be a worthy goal. But it also requires considerable preparation time, library and research facilities, and page space or air time to do justice to complexities. There also must be an audience that has the interest as well as the leisure to read and listen. When these conditions exist, the product is a legitimate supplying of a consumer demand. When the conditions do not exist, social science journalism reflects a failure in the market economics of the news business and the degree to which reporters set their own agendas.[14]

---

[14]Stephen Hess, *The Washington Reporters* (Washington, D.C.: Brookings Institution, 1981), p. 119.

One of the "economic" topics that arose in the symposium discussion was the growing concentration of media ownership and the shrinking number of newspapers. This was dramatized in the summer of 1981 by the demise of the *Washington Star*, which left the nation's capital with only one local daily newspaper. (Of course, out-of-town newspapers circulate in Washington, and there are several papers that serve Washington suburbs.) A number of other dailies, particularly afternoon papers, were reported to be in dire financial positions.

The *Star* died despite the financial backing of Time Inc., which bought the newspaper in 1978. Nine years earlier, the *Star* had absorbed another paper, the *Washington Daily News*. Circulation, which peaked at 418,000 after the *Star* bought the *News*, had plummeted to 323,000 when Time Inc. announced the *Star*'s closing. A Time executive, when asked why his company had not been able to save the *Star*, responded with one word—"ads."[15] The *Star* attracted only about 25 percent of the advertising linage, despite lower rates than those of the *Washington Post*. The *Star* was said to be losing $20 million annually, and simply could not compete with the *Post* for advertisers.[16]

The decline in the number of newspapers has been accompanied by the increase in newspaper chain ownership. About 62 percent of the nation's dailies and weeklies are owned by corporate chains. Chains control more than 72 percent of all daily circulation. Of more significance perhaps, the four largest chains account for more than one-fourth of all papers sold. The twenty-five largest chains control more than 50 percent of all daily circulation. Some of the largest corporate groups are also involved in other media areas. For example, many of these corporations or their affiliates have been acquiring large numbers of cable television systems. Time Inc. owns both American Television and Communications (ATC), the largest cable operator, and Home Box Office, the most successful pay-TV program service. There seems to be a clear pattern of concentrated ownership in areas of the newer communications technology. Cable television is becoming dominated by a small number of companies. Ten companies serve more

---

[15]Ray White, "The Washington Star 1852-1981," *Washington Journalism Review* 3, no. 7 (September 1981): 11.

[16]*Washington Post*, July 24, 1981.

than half the nation's cable subscribers.

The point is made that conglomerate ownership is not an inherently bad situation. For example, large corporations can provide greater financial stability for newspapers, and, in some cases, greater independence. But, as Hodding Carter argued during the symposium, the people running media enterprises now "are big-power people." He said, "They increasingly represent not the communities in which they operate, but a megacommunity simply divorced from the knowledge, the concerns, even the economic conditions of most of the people they serve."

Many of the large media interests have the resources to be doing much more, and seem primarily concerned with the profit ledger and content with the status quo. According to Carter, "the answer to the problems of irresponsibility in press performance is, in fact, more competition, more freedom, more press, more diversity."

George Christian concurred, "Our danger lies not in the competitive nature of the media, but in the possibility of concentrated media power."

The First Amendment

Daniel Schorr, differing with some of the panelists, said the First Amendment *is* in trouble today. It is in trouble, said Schorr, "because the industry that the First Amendment was created to protect has grown far beyond the bounds of what it was meant to protect."

While Schorr sees the First Amendment being stretched to protect a vast media establishment, Douglass Cater commented that over two centuries, the First Amendment has already "been stretched beyond almost any recognition of its literal words."

Legal experts at the symposium assessed recent court decisions and had their own views of possible threats to the First Amendment. Archibald Cox said, "Despite the moaning and groaning of the press, its freedom under the First Amendment is much greater today than it has ever been before in our history."

Another legal scholar, Edward Barrett, Jr., said, "I find it ironical that the established press, one of the most powerful institutions in modern society, and well able to fight its own battles in the political arenas, has an apparently insatiable appetite for constitutional guarantees." However,

Professor Barrett cautioned that if the press goes too far in insisting on a constitutionally privileged position, this will create "almost irresistible...pressure for government controls to ensure that the press acts fairly." Barrett said, "The electronic media have paid the price of some government controls in return for exclusive privileges to use the nation's airways. The print media may be next and, if so, the First Amendment as we know it will not have survived."

Judge Thomas Gee said, however, that the protection of the First Amendment is going to continue to exist because the courts are going to see that it does.

While Judge Gee pronounced the First Amendment "in good health" and "in danger only from excesses and...not really in much danger from that," Professor Dwight Teeter offered the view that the First Amendment is always in trouble. He said it is "the nature of the situation" and added: "Things wax and wane, but we cannot ever say that any freedom is won once and for all."

Columnist Joseph Kraft emphasized that he was not moaning and groaning (Archibald Cox's terms) about press freedom. "I do not think the free press is under any serious difficulty now. I think we are alive and well and eating our attackers for breakfast every day."

But Kraft said he was concerned about self-righteousness within the press. Marianne Means agreed: the press is alive and well—but not perfect.

A few weeks after the symposium, Anthony Lewis wrote in the *New York Times* about the danger of excessive pride or arrogance among journalists: "In our case it is a constitutional hubris, a belief that the First Amendment gives journalism an exalted status. It is in particular a belief that the Constitution gives us a right to use anonymous sources without being called to account."[17]

The Media Performance

Television newsman Jim Lehrer made concluding remarks at the symposium and he confronted this issue, saying that journalists have somehow gotten it into their heads "that we are truly the special people of this world,...above all laws, above all rules that the rest of society has to play by." He said, "We are not the special

---

[17]Lewis, "First Amendment Hubris."

people of the world; only our work is."

Lehrer said that journalists need to explain better why it is necessary to rely on confidential sources in some cases—cases that may affect the public's rights more than they affect the reporters.

But, Lehrer said, "We have got to stop defending the indefensible. We have to acknowledge our mistakes and correct them as best we can. We have got to clean up our own ethics. We have to eliminate every smell of double standard. We have to expose ourselves to the same kind of public scrutiny that we demand of every other segment of public life."

Many of the participants referred to this need for criticism and internal and external assessment of the media. Some of the recent instances of press "irresponsibility" and controversial coverage have brought on a wave of such assessment and consideration of the media's role and performance. The symposium provided a provocative example of what should be an ongoing examination of the interaction between the press, government, politics, and the public. It also provided a reaffirmation of the vital role that the media play in our society.

HOYT PURVIS

1
Can the First Amendment Survive a Free Press?

Opening Remarks by JOHN B. CONNALLY

If, indeed, we are a free society, if, indeed, we are a free people, then we are going to continue to have a free press, provided we have a responsible press. Whether or not we continue to be a free people and a free society will be determined by each generation and how it succeeds. And I well understand the Constitution and its guarantees, but that Constitution is a piece of paper. That paper is as meaningful as society makes it meaningful.

We live in a time of a rapidly changing world. No one of us can be certain that the changes will not be so violent and so pervasive as to overturn what we believe to be our inalienable right to life, liberty, and the pursuit of happiness.

Now, let's think back over the last thirty-five years about some of the changes that have buffeted and encompassed this world. Then let's try to translate that in terms of whether we will continue to have a free and responsible press in the future.

What has happened since the end of World War II? What has happened in the last thirty-five years? What effect has it had on us? Too few of us stop and think and try to analyze the impact of these changes. The end of World War II saw the end of the colonial empires that had basically dominated the world for three-hundred years. The end of the colonial empires meant the end of that colonial expansion. Those empires, for better or for worse, had built international trade and commerce. They had educated. They had brought civilization to all the continents of the earth. But at the end of World War II, the British and other colonial empires no longer existed. And today, in my opinion, the British suffer greatly because they have not learned to live without an empire. That is true of a great many other countries in the world: they have not learned to live without an empire.

What else has happened in those thirty-five years?

Thirty-five years ago, the United States stood at the absolute apex of its power, unquestionably the strongest military nation on earth, unquestionably the strongest economic force on earth. We and we alone had the atom bomb thirty-five years ago. We could have dominated any nation. We could have subjugated any people. We could have conquered any land, more certain and more surely than any other civilization that ever existed, but we chose not to do it.

Since that time, what has happened? We have, in the view of many, become a second-rate power. Thirty-five years ago, the economic vitality of this nation was such that we shared the largess and the bounty and the strength of this land with other nations around the world in order to help rebuild those nations and rehabilitate their people. And out of that rehabilitation process rose powers, economic powers that today are challenging us—the Germans, the Japanese, and others all around the globe.

So conditions have changed, changed dramatically and drastically. During these thirty-five years, we fought two wars we dared not win, that we feared to win. During these thirty-five years, we've seen a turbulence and a turmoil in this country and all over the world in many facets of our society and our life. We've undergone a racial revolution. We've undergone a revolution of youth. We've undergone a revolution of religion. We are now still in the throes of another revolution, arising out of the rights of women. This is a very pervasive movement that had its beginning here and will now spread throughout all the lands of the earth—and it's going to have a profound impact as it has here. It's going to change society.

Now, through all this turbulence, through all this turmoil, Americans have become more and more concerned about their government, their leaders. They have lost confidence in their political leadership. They've lost confidence in the press. They've lost confidence in institutions for many reasons, not the least of which is that the press all too frequently says that good news is no news; only bad news is news.

All too frequently we've given over to sensationalism. We've become worshippers of athletes and entertainers, largely because, sheerly because of publicity. Consider the devotees of an Elvis Presley or a John Lennon. When John Lennon was tragically assassinated, I suspect he got more ink than any other human being in the last twenty years, and why? What had he done? Elvis Presley, a great entertainer, a great singer. We still have movies, plays, television that show all about him, yet, in the final analysis, he killed himself with drugs. He was a drug addict. He was not someone to be emulated. He was not someone to be admired. He was not someone to hold up to the youth of America as someone that they should try to be like.

We all too frequently lose perspective. We look for instantaneous gratification of our desires, not our needs but our desires. We are in a turbulent world, and what is happening today is a result of it. We've reached the point where people everywhere feel they can take the law into their own hands to redress any real or imaginary wrong that they have suffered. We've reached the point where we have a rising crime rate, unprecedented in the history of this country. We have a situation where people are fearful. They're fearful to go outdoors, they're fearful to help law enforcement officers.

We've reached a point—though this is hopefully beginning to turn—where all of the forces of this government are always on the side of protecting the rights of the criminal. Rarely is a great deal of attention paid to the victims. We have a situation in which the press has changed dramatically.

In the last thirty-five years, we've put a man on the moon. We've done things that none of us ever conceived we would do, but probably the most significant change that has occurred in the last thirty-five years and perhaps in the last two- or three-hundred years has been the advent of television.

Prior to the advent of television, what did we have? We had a number of newspapers. We had radio stations. Radio itself is a fairly modern invention. It played no part in the political life of this nation, the entertainment life of the nation, until the late 1920s. It was not a force in America. Television certainly was not a force until well after World War II. Prior to that time, we had the newspapers and their sphere of influence. And that is not to say that in the days of the newspaper czars—the William Randolph Hearsts, men of that type—that we did not have a press, at least in some cases, that was highly motivated, politically partisan, personally dominated by individuals. Chains were, individual newspapers were, but, nevertheless, the extent of their influence was limited. Whether you liked a particular paper or not, you could always console yourself with the thought that its coverage was limited, and its influence was limited, therefore, by that coverage.

No one periodical in this nation has or ever had the pervasive influence that we see today with the advent of television. Today, there is almost a monopoly of news coverage. Approximately three-fourths of all the people in America today get what news they receive and what knowledge they have from watching television news. That news is basically dominated by five institutions: three networks and two newspapers. Actually, I should say seven: three networks, two newspapers, and two wire services—CBS, ABC, NBC, the *New York Times*, the *Washington Post*, the Associated Press, and United Press International.

Every morning, the television editors wake up, read the *New York Times* to see what is being played in the *Times*. They then begin to talk with their various editors. They talk to the reporters in Washington. They begin to set up what is going to be played on the evening telecast. And that is why every evening, day in and day out, you'll see the same stories almost in sequence, one, two, three, four, on all three networks—because they are basically following the lead of the *New York Times* or the *Washington Post*, with an occasional lead, depending on the breaking stories, out of the Associated Press or UPI.

Now, this is pervasive. This goes into every home in America. This has a profound influence on America. It changes the thoughts of Americans. It changes the reactions of people to circumstances and to events, depending on how those events are portrayed on television.

Will we continue to have a free press? We will continue to have a free press so long as we have a responsible press. But a responsible press cannot be negative in its character. A responsible press, in my judgment, cannot long adopt the attitude that the only news is bad news.

How long can a free people be bombarded with the evil, the sensational, the spectacular, the bad, without assuming and believing that we're all rotten to the core? If you ask the reporters themselves, they will say to you—and the studies that have been made of the reporters clearly indicate this—that the least interesting subject to them is economics. They are all interested in diplomatic service. They are all interested in the White House. They're interested in the

Congress. They're interested in every type of journalism except economics. That evokes the least interest of all, and yet that is the most fundamental of all.

Are we going to have a free and responsible press? We are if the universities and the schools of journalism start teaching something about economics, something about what this country is, and something about the economic system that prevails in this country. We are so long as the networks make up their mind that they are not God-given institutions. They are commercial enterprises. They are profit-making organizations of the highest order, in terms of return on equity, return on capital, and total dollars earned.

There's nothing wrong with that. That's what this country is all about, profitmaking. They ought to make a profit. There's nothing wrong with it, but it is significant that this is one of the few countries on earth where it's permitted.

The television networks have to understand that they are going to continue to be free to operate on public airways and make profits, whatever they are, so long as they maintain some degree of objectivity, so long as they understand that they have a responsibility to do more than give you thirty seconds of news about some event. Television may well determine whether or not we remain a free people. Nothing is more critical to us in the dissemination of information than television.

Throughout my life, I have been privileged to know most of the great reporters, some not so great, some highly professional, and some not so professional. They are no different from anyone else. They're all human, and they are all biased like the rest of us. But they disavow any bias. They assume a purity, a pristine purity that destroys their credibility and almost everything else.

Reporters are human beings, and they in their writings inevitably reflect their own background, their own experience, as well they should. We should not ask them to be superpeople. They're not superpeople. They're like all of us. They reflect their home towns, they reflect their educations, they reflect their experiences, whatever they might be. And that's good, so long as they don't assume that they are part of an elitist group that knows better what's good for us than we do.

I suppose if I had to pick out individuals I had no great respect for in the journalism profession, I could probably find five. Over the years, again beginning back in 1939 when I first went to Washington as a young man, twenty-two years old, I've seen some of the great reporters. I've listened to them. I've watched them. This dates back to the time when radio was really beginning to have an impact under President Roosevelt.

I remember when Drew Pearson was in his heyday, when he and Bob Allen had the Merry-Go-Round in 1939, 1940, before Bob Allen went off to the wars.* I remember when Marshall McNeil,† whom I thought was one of the toughest reporters that I ever dealt with in my life, was running around the capitol. I won't attempt to name them all.

All of my life, personal and professional and political, I've known most of the reporters. I have formed an affection for a great many. I have admired many more, and I have disliked very few. I think by and large they try to do a workman-like job. I think part of the problem in the journalism profession, at least this was true until very recently, was that it probably was as badly paid as any profession in America. Youngsters coming out of school did far worse in the field of journalism than anywhere else. It was notoriously bad pay whether you worked for a newspaper or a radio station or one of the wire services.

Most of the reporters were all young people because they were coming out of school and they were getting their jobs. They were getting responsibilities for writing stories.

By their very nature, young people are rebellious. Their every instinct is to be against institutions and things as they are. Young people want to change things. They want to shake up things. Regardless of what exists, they're against it, and much of this is reflected in the reporting that comes out of the young people, who are not prepared professionally or educationally, really, to deal with most of the subjects with which they have to deal. Now, as they grow older, as they get more experience, as they get more training, as they move up in the ranks of the profession, obviously this is no longer true. Obviously, today you have

---

*Robert S. Allen and Drew Pearson wrote the syndicated column, "Washington Merry-Go-Round," from 1932 to 1942. Pearson continued the column on his own, and later Allen also had a syndicated column. Jack Anderson joined Pearson as a reporter in 1947 and in a jointly syndicated column in 1965 before Pearson died in 1969.

†Marshall McNeil was a long-time Washington correspondent for the Scripps-Howard newspapers, and covered the Texas Congressional delegation.

people reporting in the scientific field who are superb. You have those in the economic field that are unequaled. You have political and diplomatic reporters who are as knowledgeable as any Secretary of State or anyone serving in that department of government.

I'm not talking just about government; I'm talking about reporting of all events in America. I'm talking about what is going to assure a free and a responsible press, and that is essentially the continued faith of the American people in this profession, in the reporting, in the news that they get, in the belief that this news is not slanted, that it is not doctored, that it basically is as nonpartisan and as objective as it can be made. But I think it needs to go beyond that.

I think the world is in such a difficult situation today, the forces are so complex, that the American people do not feel that they understand or that they are being told the truth. Therefore they're not willing to do anything.

We shouldn't have an energy crisis in America, not at all. A moment ago, I pointed out many things that had happened in the last thirty-five years. There is one other thing that has happened in the last thirty-five years that brings us into a dramatic posture — thirty-five years ago you couldn't give away natural gas. Thirty-five years ago, there were no pipelines. Thirty-five years ago, if you could find a market for natural gas, it was three, four cents per thousand mcf. It was being flared all over this state and all over the oil-producing states in the Union. But in thirty-five years, we have gone from an overabundance, from the point where gas was a commodity for which there was no market, to the point where it now provides about a quarter of the energy needs of this nation. We've developed shortages. We've seen the rise of the OPEC nations. The whole world has changed, and what has been the result?

The result has been that we have seen the most massive shift of resources that ever has occurred in the history of the world. Now, that means something to you and me. We have seen in the past thirty-five years a falling apart, a deterioration, and ultimately the collapse of the whole international monetary system. That means something to you and me, but the average American does not understand what it means simply because no one has ever taken the time to tell him. Yet it is important because it determines the value of his money, it determines the value of commodities, it determines the economic vitality of this nation.

In 1971, when we were really in the midst of the collapse of the international monetary agreement that had been established at Bretton Woods during World War II, there was no understanding on the part of many of the reporters in America of what was really at stake in trying to bring about a change in the comparative relationship of currencies in the world. But, I assure you, the other countries understood it. They've gone through it many times. We had never gone through it. We were witnessing things for the first time in America.

We had assumed after the war that this great economic strength of ours and military strength of ours would continue unchallenged and undiminished. That is what most of us thought. All of us lived under the assumption that we would always have cheap energy because we had had it. We made no preparations for what was to come. And today, we're vulnerable. We're enormously vulnerable. Why? Because the American people were not informed of what was to be an impending crisis. If there had not been an October War, 1973, that time of crisis would have been projected into the future, but that war occurred and the crisis came, and it is going to come again and we're going to have a crisis in strategic metals and materials. We're having a crisis now in many aspects of the economic life of this nation—in steel, in automobiles, in textiles, and a great many other things. Why? Because in this free society, we never take time to understand what is happening to us. We never understand the real forces at play. We never understand that the extent we are willing to plan for the future is ultimately going to determine what kind of a society we're going to have. There is no hope for a free press unless we continue as a free people, free economically, not just free legally. There is no society on earth in which you have personal freedom and press freedom without economic freedom.

These are the things we have to concern ourselves with. What kind of a nation are we going to live in ten, fifteen, twenty years from now? What kind of a world will we have? Will we be able to cope with it? Will a representative government with checks and counterchecks, with balances and counterbalances be able to survive? Will it be able to respond to the exigencies of the times in which we live? Will it be able to react promptly and quickly and dramatically enough and drastically enough to cope with events precipitated by the other nations around the world?

These are the things we have to concern ourselves with. The world is not going to move at our pace, not any longer. We may have to march to someone else's drummer, and we certainly will if we don't anticipate what is ahead of us and what we need to do in order to protect our own well-being and our own economic system.

Most of those in the press take the position that it is not their responsibility to defend this economic system. Then whose is it? They exist because of it. They prosper because of this economic system.

Truly, I'm not prepared to defend this system as being perfect, but I think it is a little better than trying to read *Pravda* every day. I think it is a little better than we find in most other countries around the world. I don't know of a better system. I think if anyone knows of a better system, if the press has a better system, they ought to be proposing it.

I think it is the responsibility of the press to defend a few things in this country and not just to attack them. I think it is the press's responsibility to explain a few things and not try to destroy them. I think it is its responsibility not to be sensational but rather to be studied in its approach to many of the problems of this country. Only then can we build a degree of confidence in the minds of the American people to sustain us in a time of crisis. In a time of prosperity, in a time of well-being, of relaxation, and of peace and tranquility, we have no problems, but we're not going to live in that kind of world.

We have unleashed forces in this world that are certain to provide an ever-changing and an ever-turbulent world for the next half century and perhaps far, far longer into the future. We're witnessing today developing nations of the world on the verge of a collapse. Why? Because of the cost of energy. The developing nations to whom we have extended a helping hand over these many years are today bankrupt. The Third World countries en masse can no longer even meet their interest payments, much less principal payments on their external debts. Why? Largely because of energy costs.

What are we doing about it? We're not even looking after our own needs. We're not even developing our own resources. We're permitting a handful of nations, the OPEC countries, to determine the economic well-being of nations and the prosperity and the well-being of billions of people on earth. That's the impact. That's the result.

We have to understand not just what occurred yesterday and this evening, not just a thirty-second blurb on television about what happened today, but what the consequences are of the basic underlying forces that affect this nation and its well-being and its security and its survivability. If the press wants to remain a free press—and we all want it to remain a free press—it must be responsible enough to devote some of its time, some of its energies, to trying to explain to the American people the forces that are at play in the world and the impact that those forces are going to have on each one of us, in order that we can have an informed judgment.

No representative government, in my opinion, can long survive without having an informed electorate. That's our problem: to inform, to advise, and to educate. That also is going to have to be the responsibility of a continuing free press.

Panel Statements

ARTHUR GINSBURG, Moderator: *"Congress shall make no law abridging the freedom of speech or of the press."*

Simple words, beautifully written, right to the point. The Americans who drafted those words knew firsthand the benefits of a free press. From the very beginning, it was the press which provided the means of communicating the defiance necessary to arouse public support for the revolution and to galvanize public opinion in favor of a concerted stand against the British. But also from the very conception of the First Amendment, neither newspaper editors nor political leaders were very clear about what freedom of the press really meant.

You might think that after all that experience with the use of the press for political purposes the meaning would be clear, but historians indicate otherwise. It may not have meant what we generally take for granted, that newspapers or other media are completely immune from penalties for criticism of the government.

Even James Alexander, the staunch defender of Peter Zenger, stated that "to infuse in the minds of people an ill opinion of a just administration is a crime that deserves no mercy." And it is a fact that some of the political leaders of the time, the very people, by the way, who badly needed and extolled the virtues of the free press, became very intolerant of criticism when they themselves assumed power.

Much, therefore, depends on which side of the fence you are on. Attacks on the press and the media from those in power have continued in direct and some quite indirect ways right up until the present time.

Now, while the meaning of the First Amendment is not always clear, it seems to me very clear that the press fervently believes—and it has its supporters on the bench, though very few I might say—that any restrictions on free communication present an inherent danger to a free society. Ideally, the press wants no restraints, so that, as envisaged by the First Amendment philosophers, there can be a dissemination of diverse viewpoints and information on public affairs, with an informed electorate receiving that healthy exposure to diverse viewpoints.

Of course, that is the ideal situation, but public opinion, and yes, even the law are subject to cyclical changes which are not always easily perceived. Certainly, there are periodic swings from left to right or right to left and back again, from greater to lesser freedoms of speech and expression.

One must be mindful of changes in Supreme Court membership and resulting historical fluctuations in legal interpretations of the First Amendment. Considered in this way, the First Amendment can be viewed as a very fragile few lines indeed. It is under continuous attack from several sources and has to continually fight off problems involving libel, invasions of privacy, even security of the United States. Can the First Amendment survive a totally free press?

Consider this: Did the framers of the Constitution have in mind only prohibitions against prior restraint? They seemed to be perfectly willing, as several statements of the time from Benjamin Franklin, Thomas Jefferson, and many others show, to allow punishment for press activity following publication. Looking at it another way, is the press today claiming rights beyond those that were envisaged by the framers of the Constitution?

It has been said that the press claims many privileges in addition to those that ordinary citizens have under the claim of free speech. Prior cases have held there is a right to gather news, but the press has no greater rights than citizens have.

A recent case, *Richmond Newspapers* v. *Virginia*,* went even further, holding that the press is a stand-in for the public and that the right to attend criminal trials is implicit in the guarantees of the First Amendment. This, I might say in passing, in part made up for what the press views as the horrors of *Gannett* v. *DePasquale*,† which held that criminal pretrial proceedings could be closed to the public under certain circumstances. In that regard, briefly, Supreme Court Justice William Brennan, in a speech in 1979,‡ stated he believed the credibility of the press was impaired because of its excessive reactions to court decisions such as the *Lando*§ case, which journalists saw as hampering the press. "Either the press," he said, "like other institutions, will recognize that it must accommodate a variety of important social interests which the sad complexity of our society makes inevitable or it will face a shrill and impotent isolation." Strong words indeed.

When the press enjoys victories such as the *Richmond* case and as media changes due to rapidly advancing new technologies, as Governor Connally said, enabling it to become even more pervasive in today's life, will the free press behave in such a manner that it will force the courts to reduce rather than enlarge the scope of the First Amendment?

---

*On July 2, 1980, the Supreme Court, 7-1, in *Richmond Newspapers, Inc.* v. *Virginia* (448 U.S. 555, 100 U.S.C. 2814 [1980]), concluded that the right of the public and press to attend criminal trials is guaranteed under the First and Fourteenth amendments. The decision was hailed as a major victory by press organizations. The Court reversed a Virginia Supreme Court ruling that upheld exclusion of the public and press from a murder trial.

†On July 2, 1979, one year before the *Richmond* decision, the Supreme Court had ruled, 5-4, in *Gannett Co., Inc.* v. *DePasquale* (443 U.S. 368, 99 S. Ct. 2898 [1979]), that members of the public had no constitutional right to attend pretrial hearings in a criminal case. The Court held that the Sixth Amendment's public trial guarantee does not give the press and public right of access to a pretrial suppression hearing that was closed by the trial court with the agreement of both prosecution and defense, since the pretrial guarantee is for the benefit of the defendant alone.

‡Justice William J. Brennan, Jr., spoke at the dedication of the Samuel I. Newhouse Law Center at Rutgers University, October 18, 1979. Excerpts from his address were published in *Columbia Journalism Review*, January/February 1980, pp. 59-62.

§On April 18, 1979, the Supreme Court ruled, 6-3, in *Herbert* v. *Lando* (441 U.S. 153, 99 S. Ct. 1635 [1979]), that journalists defending their work against libel action can be required to disclose opinions they held during the editorial process and their reasons for making specific news judgments. The Court said this is necessary to enable public figures to satisfy the heavy evidentiary burden of demonstrating reckless or knowing disregard for the truth. Former Army officer Lt. Col. Anthony Herbert had contended that he was libeled on a CBS Television "Sixty Minutes" program, produced by Barry Lando.

Another problem: When the press is totally free, if it ever will be, will there be a backlash from the public and ultimate pressure on the courts when it is realized that the press and all media may be dominated by a few Ma Bell-type conglomerates and that access to media can be highly restricted?

To paraphrase A. J. Liebling,* freedom of the press is great when you have one. Will there be pressures on the First Amendment regarding access, even overthrowing the *Tornillo*† case, which stated that there is no fairness doctrine or right of reply regarding newspapers? The same problems exist in radio and television, a subject near and dear to my heart. If conglomerates gobble up the media, will the Supreme Court stick with its views expressed in the 1969 *Red Lion* decision,‡ holding that the public's rights are paramount and supersede the broadcasters' First Amendment privileges? Put another way, will the public's First Amendment rights come before the broadcasters'?

EDWARD L. BARRETT, JR.: I found the question that was posed for discussion difficult to understand. I decided to rephrase this question into a form calculated to provoke a response from the representatives of the press.

---

*A. J. Liebling was a reporter and for many years a leading press critic, writing the "Wayward Press" column in *New Yorker* magazine. Liebling, who died in 1963, was the author of numerous books, including *The Press*, originally published in 1961.

†A Florida statute provided that if a newspaper attacked the character or official record of a candidate for public office, the newspaper must, upon request of the candidate and without cost, permit the injured party the right to publish a reply. In 1972, the *Miami Herald* refused such a request from Pat Tornillo, candidate for the state legislature, who had been attacked in *Herald* editorials and accused of failing to file a required list of campaign contributors. A local trial court held that the law was in violation of the First Amendment and refused to enforce it. The Florida Supreme Court reversed the lower-court ruling. The *Miami Herald* appealed the decision to the U.S. Supreme Court, which, in June 1974, unanimously reversed the Florida ruling. In *Miami Herald* v. *Tornillo* (418 U.S. 713, 94 S. Ct. 2831 [1979]), Chief Justice Warren Burger said, "A responsible press is an undoubtedly desirable goal, but press responsibility is not mandated by the Constitution and like many other virtues it cannot be legislated."

‡In a unanimous decision in 1969, the Supreme Court, in *Red Lion Broadcasting Co.* v. *FCC* (395 U.S. 367, 89 S. Ct. 1794 [1969]), held that maligned individuals deserve the right of reply and that the public has the right to hear opposing views. A small Pennsylvania radio station had challenged an FCC ruling requiring it to provide free reply time to author Fred Cook, who had been attacked by evangelist Billy James Hargis on a program paid for by the Christian Crusade. In its decision, the Supreme Court upheld the Fairness Doctrine and its "personal attack" rules. Some have suggested that the case was a hollow victory for advocates of free access because it contributed to a sharp curtailment of broadcast time for controversial commentary.

Will the nation continue to tolerate the First Amendment as we know it? If it is interpreted to give license to the press to intrude into the functioning of government and the lives of individuals, free of the normal legal constraints applied to ensure the protection of important public and private interests, I find it ironical that the established press, one of the most powerful institutions in modern society, and well able to fight its own battles in the political arenas, has an apparently insatiable appetite for constitutional guarantees.

Unsatisfied with half a century of constitutional adjudication that has accorded it a high degree of protection against governmental controls, the press greets each decision that refuses to extend those protections even further as an unwarranted restriction of freedom of the press, as a retreat from the essential values of the First Amendment.

The press is possessed of unique advantages in the political arena which shuns legislation and pays lawyers to importune the Supreme Court. Its basic position appears to be that the First Amendment should accord to the press complete freedom without legal responsibility, assuring the public it will not abuse the freedom given. Yet later in this symposium, members of the press will discuss the interesting question, How responsible can a free and competitive press be?

The press has long since won the most important constitutional battles. The government cannot prevent the press from printing whatever information it has. Fortunately for our democratic system, the press is almost wholly unrestrained in its role as a critic of government. It can speak and write about government in measured or unmeasured terms, subject only to the quite remote possibility of libel verdicts when it intentionally or recklessly makes false statements defaming public officials.

Yet the press wants more. It seeks almost total immunity from even defending libel suits, heedless of the reputational and privacy interests of others. It seeks constitutional immunity for press representatives from being compelled, as other citizens are, to provide information which may be vital to the prosecution or defense in criminal cases or to the enforcement of court decrees. It asserts immunity from discovery of editorial processes because, the press says, frank discussion among reporters and editors will be dampened and sound editorial judgment endangered if such exchanges are subject to inquiry by defamation plaintiffs. But at the same time, it seeks a constitutional right of press access to governmental information, including exchanges among governmental officials.

The danger, of course, is that creation of such a constitutionally privileged position for the press will make almost irresistible the pressure for government controls to ensure that the press acts fairly in its role as a trustee for the public.

The electronic media have paid the price of some government controls in return for exclusive privileges to use the nation's airways. The print media may be next and, if so, the First Amendment as we know it will not have survived.

DOUGLASS CATER: President Johnson used to tell a story about the farmer—I believe he was a Texas farmer—who was asked where he stood on a controversial issue, and he said, "I ain't made up my mind, but when I do I'm prepared to be gall-durned bitter." This is the attitude with which I approach this controversial subject. Perhaps my trouble is I've thought about it for too long and have become addled in the process.

Briefly, I would like to pose about four or five stark propositions and see to what extent they elicit controversy or agreement.

The first is in direct answer to the question before us. The First Amendment, over nearly two centuries, has been stretched beyond almost any recognition of its literal words by efforts to interpret it. Our living Constitution, that which the courts and the condoned practices of the nation have set, has obliged us to climb out on a good many limbs in trying to interpret freedom of the press. I think it would be a great mistake—and I think I agree with Professor Barrett—to rely over-heavily on the courts to give constant and central interpretation to freedom of the press.

Almost any court decision can be pushed to absurdity—particularly, I would say, the decisions that go to the search for malicious intent on the part of the journalist or the editor in the publication of a story. I see no real opportunities for freedom in over-reliance on the courts.

My next proposition is that politicians are by their very nature very poorly equipped to define press freedom. They are a different breed of fish. They do not look on the basic workings of society in the same way that journalists do. I think the first steps toward a closed society comes with political efforts to define what is news and what it should contain.

The next proposition is that this problem is going to get bigger before it gets smaller. The technology has brought the potential for the fissioning of communications, and the increased competition among the media is going to lead to increased playing on the borderlines of what is freedom under the First Amendment.

The final two brief propositions:

Public opinion, at least as interpreted by a recent, very interesting study by Dan Yankelovich and Associates, has been remarkably tolerant of press freedom. Yet public opinion also expects the press to be fair and responsible. I would submit this Yankelovich study to the reading of all journalism students because it is, I think, a very useful inquiry into public opinion. Our task is to determine how the common sense of public opinion can prevail in this tricky area without excessive reliance on courts or politicians.

One last point: Our founding fathers never intended that there be no price to pay for free press. They went back to Blackstone, who said, "If a free man publishes what is improper, mischievous, or illegal, he must take the consequences of his own temerity."* And Ben Franklin, who was both a founding father and a publisher, said, "The press should have freedom to publish what it likes so long as the public has the freedom to break the editor's pate."

ARCHIBALD COX: I come to our topic by singling out the contribution of the press to the workings of representative government. It has other functions, but it seems to me that is the central and most important one. And as Governor Connally said, the role of the press in making democracy work, if it does work, is even more central than before.

Despite the moaning and the groaning of the press, its freedom under the First Amendment is much greater today than it has ever been before in our history. The right to publish what information you have or comments you have to make belongs to all of us as individuals and to the press equally, and surely should be maintained. It is when we get to the area of indirect interference with publication that the

---

*Sir William Blackstone (1723-1780) was an English jurist whose *Commentaries* were fundamental to the study of English law.

claims of the press often become claims of special privilege and become necessarily controversial.

I go back far enough to remember when newspaper publishers, the American Newspaper Publishers Association, were claiming that they should not have to comply with the minimum wage law and pay reporters as much as forty cents an hour because that would interfere with the amount of money that they had to spend on publication. And perhaps that is why I am a little skeptical of their claims for freedom from anything that regulates them in any way that may interfere with publication.

There are two critical areas today in which I think the law is in the process of development and which are of enormous importance. First, does the press have a special right to information about what is going on in government and does the First Amendment give it that right?

If there is any right of that kind, it seems to me it must be a right of the press as the representatives of the rest of us in that we all cannot have an endless right to information about government at any time. I think that is an issue that could be discussed at some length.

Second, the great question that has been mentioned several times is this: What about rights of access *to* the press, particularly to television, where, as Governor Connally observed, three networks presently dominate?

I suspect that the law will not indefinitely follow the notion that there is complete editorial license, unless perhaps new technological developments enormously diversify the channels of public information, and then the problem would happily go away.

THOMAS GEE: As the only member of the judiciary on the panel, I suppose it falls to me to take up the particular aspect of the press and the courts as they rub together.

In attempting to answer the question before us—can the First Amendment survive a free press?—I have tried to define what we mean by "free" or "free and responsible." What I have come up with is this: If by free and responsible, we mean a press which is able to do as it likes and is subject to self-imposed restraints alone, then it cannot survive. There are quite a few reasons why that sort of absolutism as regards the First Amendment simply will not wash.

In the first place, the ease of access to the ranks of the press is so great that anyone can become a member of the press from day to day. A man who has a hectograph machine is a member of the press, after all.

The second reason is that there simply, in my view, are some matters in the polity that cannot be spread all over the papers or the media every day. It is serious enough when someone takes it in mind to publish the names of overseas intelligence agents of the country; but, if someone takes it in mind to publish the geographical quadrant locations of the intercontinental ballistic missle (ICBM) silos in this country, that is a different matter. It is simply something which, it seems to me, cannot be permitted, and I do not think the courts will permit it, prior restraint or no prior restraint.

So I don't think there is much room for real absolutism and I doubt that it's really necessary. I have never lived in Britain. About as close as I have gotten to doing it is reading the *Economist*, which I do regularly, and I do not find that the *Economist* seems much more restrained than its counterparts published in this country. And yet, there is no formal First Amendment in Britain, and I am told there is even an Official Secrets Act.

I guess it is fashionable to say that "Congress shall make *no* law. . . ." That was the way Justice Black used to say it. But it is also possible to say, "*Congress* shall make no law. . . ." So I do not think we really get much help out of literalism.

I think the real informing spirit of the First Amendment was very much in line with Ben Franklin's remark about broken heads, something in line with the Spanish proverb that says, "Take what you will, God says, and pay for it."

JOSEPH KRAFT: It is probably singularly inappropriate that the luck of the alphabet leads me to be the first working journalist to comment, because I am not going to fit the stereotype that has been set up by all these would-be attackers taking shots at the press. I am not going to moan and I am not going to groan. I am not going to gripe and I am not going to complain. It does not seem to me that anybody has said anything very harsh, sharp, revolutionary, anything that I cannot live with. I am going to try to say a word about why I think many of the things that have been said are true. I am going to try and say a word about why I think the problem is not so much the First Amendment but an underlying condition that causes us to behave the way we do with respect to the First Amendment.

First, let me say that I do think the First Amendment can easily survive a free press. The answer to the question, it seems to me, is clearly yes. I do not think the free press is under any serious difficulty now. I think we are alive and well and eating our attackers for breakfast every day.

I tend to agree with everything that has been said about our disposition to overstate our claims. I think we do it in the libel field, as in the *Lando* case. I think we do it in the field of access to information. If anything happens that we do not like, we say it is going to have a chilling effect. It is almost sure to have a chilling effect on the freedom of the press. I would like to ask the question, Why? and I think it has something to do with a point that Governor Connally was making a little bit earlier.

Among the many really dramatic changes that have taken place even in my brief lifetime, among the many dramatic changes that have taken place recently, has been the enormous change in the status of those of us in the media. We are much better paid than we used to be. We are much better educated than we used to be. We have much more prestige than we used to have. We are much better known. Some of us, indeed, are celebrities. There usually goes with that kind of rise in status an increase in self confidence. I think that has happened with us.

I think we are full of ourselves. I think we are, to use a word that has come into vogue recently, narcissistic. And when you are narcissistic in our business, you tend to think you are not only right about what happens but, in fact, you make things happen. And you can find plenty of people in our business who think we made the Vietnam War stop or made the Watergate investigation happen. You can find people who think Walter Cronkite made peace between Israel and Egypt. I think we tend to lose sight of the limited role we play. I think you can see that every day. I think you could see it recently when Bill Moyers, in denouncing what I think was probably a badly conceived State Department decision to cut off a debate, said that the climate of the

1950s had returned to Washington.*

It is not the climate of the 1950s. That is just wrong. There is a certain self-righteousness on our part, and I think it finds expression in our pushing too far the question of the First Amendment questions.

I would put it to you that the real problem of the press is how to cure that self-righteousness. I think maybe the only way to do it is by an increasing self-knowledge on our part. I think if we become more and more aware of how much we are dependent upon the sufferance of the public, we will perhaps do better. Sessions like this in that respect are useful. But, more important, I think we need to see that there is a difference between our interests and the national interest, that what is good for the media is not necessarily always good for the public.

We need to be more balanced. We need to see things whole, steadily. And if we do that, we will, I think, meet not only this relatively small problem of the First Amendment, but a much larger problem. I think it was the problem underlying what Governor Connally was talking about—the problem of our shallowness, indeed, the cultural shallowness of the whole country, to which we in the media contribute not a little.

MARIANNE MEANS: First of all, I certainly agree with my fellow columnist, Joe Kraft, that the press is alive and well—not perfect, but alive and well.

I would like to address myself to what I think is the thrust of Governor Connally's challenge to us, which is that we do not provide enough good news and that we do not defend the system effectively.

First of all, the reason that we like bad news, if you want to put it that way, is that it is the nature of the business. The unique events, the dramatic events—that is what, frankly, sells papers. The public is curious. It wants to know about unusual things that are going on. We are in the business of informing, and not all of us like to admit it, but we are also in the business of entertaining. Also, we do not

---

*In April 1981, the Reagan Administration denied a visa extension to Dr. Georgi A. Arbatov, Director of the Institute of the United States and Canadian Studies of the Soviet Union, and a leading Soviet expert on the United States. The denial had the effect of preventing Arbatov from participating in a televised debate on "Bill Moyers' Journal." The denial was said to be in retaliation for the refusal to allow U.S. representatives to appear on Soviet television on certain occasions.

invent these things, we merely report them.

Secondly, there is no lack of cheerleaders for our institutions. I really do not think they are suffering from not getting the word out to anybody. That is a totally different role. It is not an appropriate one for the press. The government has thousands of very well paid public relations people who crank out all kinds of information every single day.

Business has its advertising. It has its communications with the stockholders. All institutions have various forums. They have various ways of getting their word out.

Secondly, we are really a much more diverse industry than Governor Connally suggests. We are not a monolith. There is not much resemblance between the *Dallas Morning News* and the *Washington Post*. Joe Kraft and I frequently disagree on various issues. We have different views, different judgments.

There is a mix of media. Magazines approach discussing things much differently than TV; TV differently than newspapers. We are about to go into a whole new era of cable television in which a variety of new channels and information will come into our homes.

Also, I would like to suggest that when we discuss this and we say we are not doing a good enough job, would you consider the alternative? Would you have government controls, censorship? I think Richard Nixon stands as a good enough example of why we should not let government control the press.

Would you have a super-elite committee of the press set up to sort of monitor lesser colleagues? I do not think you would want that either. Governor Connally has already suggested that we are already too elite.

Would you want censorship from the courts? No, you do not want that either.

I am reminded of a story that President Johnson used to tell about two Indians. One of them invited the other to dinner. The one who was invited said, "Well, what are we going to eat?" And the first one said, "Crow." The second one said, "But that's not fit to eat." And the other one said, "It's better than owl."

Also, there is recourse against us, as has been suggested here. We do not have an absolute privilege. The courts have nibbled away at our rights in various and most justifiable ways, I think. We are also subject to intimidation. We do not like to admit this either, but it does happen.

I am reminded of a case. A *New York Times* book reviewer reviewed a book about airliner safety, specifically that of the DC-10, manufactured by McDonnell Douglas. The company had a lot of trouble with an air cargo door fault and refused to fix it, and it finally opened one time and the plane crashed and hundreds of people were killed. The book review in the *New York Times* was very enthusiastic, describing all this and McDonnell Douglas's behavior and so forth, and McDonnell Douglas sued. The case went nowhere, but the fact of the suit so intimidated other newspapers that the book review appeared in very few other papers.*

Bad publicity serves its purpose, I think. The *National Enquirer*, for instance, is going to pay a heavy price for the Carol Burnett suit, and not just the million dollars, either.†

We are not perfect. We aim for the best possible truth. I think we are the best existing organism to try to do that. Our sources are not perfect. Governments lie at times. But I am not worried about the press's getting complacent when we have controversy and discussions like this. There is no cover-up for us as there is for other institutions. We let it all hang out. Our mistakes are all out there for all to see.

HARRISON SALISBURY: I was very pleased to hear Governor Connally's remarks and his criticisms of the press because many of them are sound and many of them follow the general line of criticism that we hear in many parts of the country. I was particularly delighted because I happen to be probably the only person on the panel who is in a position to tell you what it is like to live in a country where many of

---

*On October 10, 1976, the *New York Times Book Review* printed a review by Robert Sherrill, Washington editor of the *Nation*, of two books dealing with the safety of airliners, particularly the DC-10, manufactured by McDonnell Douglas. The review was titled, "The Cheap Door that Cost 346 Lives," which referred to the 1974 crash near Paris of a Turkish Airlines DC-10. In his favorable review of the two books (*The Last Nine Minutes—The Story of Flight 981* by Moira Johnson, and *From the Tri-Motor to the DC-10: The Risk of Flying*, by Paul Eddy, Elaine Potter, and Bruce Page), Sherrill commented that "the crash needn't have happened at all" because the aircraft industry and the Federal Aviation Administration knew about the defective door design on the DC-10, but had not corrected it. Shortly after the review appeared, McDonnell Douglas filed a $25 million libel suit against the *Times* and Sherrill. However, in July 1978, McDonnell Douglas dropped the lawsuit.

†On March 26, 1981, a California Superior Court jury ruled that *National Enquirer* had libeled actress Carol Burnett in a 1976 story implying that she had been drunk and rowdy in a restaurant in Washington, D.C. The jury ordered the *Enquirer* to pay her $1.6 million in damages; the trial judge cut the award in half. *Enquirer* lawyers announced plans to appeal.

the conditions that he spoke of have been fulfilled.

I lived and worked for many years in a country where the press published only good news, no bad news. It published nothing about pop heroes, not a word about Elvis Presley, nothing about John Lennon. There was no crime news in these papers, not a line of crime news. And it was what you call a very responsible press because it never published anything without first either getting the news from the government or inquiring of the government. It published no negative news, particularly about the government. There was no sensationalism in this press, very dull headlines—hardly any headlines at all—very few pictures.

And, indeed, in regard to one of Governor Connally's remarks about the American press that I happen to agree with—that our economic reporting is very bad—practically all of the reporters in this press were steeped in economics of a particular kind. There were not very many young people working on that press, so it was not troubled by the problems of the young people who are against things, young people who want to challenge and change things. They did not have a chance. And, indeed, the staff of this press was very well paid. There were none of those problems of the American press.

Now, you know, of course, what press I am talking about. I am talking about the Russian press. I am talking about *Pravda* and *Izvestia*, and I concede that I agree with the old Russian joke, which has been told ever since the day of Lenin. *Pravda* means "truth," and *Izvestia* means "news." The Russian joke is "there is no truth in *Pravda* and there is no news in *Izvestia*."

I prefer the American press, and I think we all do. We like to criticize the press, and thank God we do criticize it. I believe in criticism. I believe in what you might call creative tension between the government and the press. I do not worry that the press is on the brink of obliteration. I think that the criticism of the press perhaps is not as strong as it ought to be and frequently does not hit us at the right points. I believe that we can only be improved and do our job better with a good and responsible public criticism feeding into what we do every day.

I happen to think that one of the high spots, perhaps the highest spot, in the great controversy between the government and the press that revolved around the Pentagon Papers, which were published by the *New York Times*, the

Washington Post, and many other newspapers, was the decision of Judge Murray Gurfein in the U.S. District Court, upholding the right of the *Times* to publish the Pentagon Papers.* And in words I wish I could quote precisely, he wound up by saying that if the free democratic process was to continue in this country, we must put up with what he called a difficult press, a ubiquitous press, and a cantankerous press. I think he was right and I think we would all agree with that. I believe if that free press is to continue, it must put up with an ubiquitous public, a difficult public, and a cantankerous public, and I think out of that we will all be the better.

KENNETH TOWERY: One good thing about being at the end of the line is that almost everything has already been said. I would not say I agree with all of it, but, nevertheless, there is no need to rehash a lot of it. I think all the bases have been covered.

My bottom line on this matter, very simply, is that I think certainly the First Amendment is going to survive a free press. I think, by and large, as has been pointed out, the First Amendment was not something that was reserved for the press itself. It is something the people want and I think as long as they want it, it is going to survive.

I think certainly, it is going to face dangers as we go along, just as any other liberty that we have will face dangers. But I think that in the final analysis it is going to survive. The things that worry me are some of the tests that are going to be made against it along the way and things of that nature. I have listened with a great deal of interest to the lawyers and to the representatives of the press. I used to think, when I was in the press every day and worrying with it, that the real danger we had in the press was just a matter of lazy reporters and dumb editors. But I think now we are going to have to add to that the danger of smart lawyers.

Panel Discussion

ARTHUR GINSBURG: We have time for discussion of some of these ideas if any of you would like to comment.

---

*The Supreme Court upheld Judge Gurfein's decision on June 30, 1971, when it ruled in the cases of *New York Times Co.* v. *U.S.* and *U.S.* v. *The Washington Post Co.* (402 U.S. 713, 91 S. Ct. 2140 [1971]) allowing the Pentagon Papers to be published.

ARCHIBALD COX: As Marianne Means and Harrison Salisbury rose to the bait put out by Governor Connally, let me rise a little bit to the bait put out by them.

First, everybody agrees that we prefer the situation of our press to the situation of the publications in Russia. Second, I think everybody agrees that any improvement in the press cannot and should not be imposed by the government, that it really puts the question in a false context to talk about criticism of the press or the faults of the press as if government should do something about it.

I quite clearly agree with the press, not the government, with respect to the Pentagon Papers, the *Progressive* magazine later, and the like.* But I am not satisfied by the answer to the Governor's criticism—that, well, it is the nature of the business. I think particularly in the case of television but somewhat in the case of the newspapers that it is not just a business of selling newspapers or a business of selling advertising and entertainment. The great revolution that has taken place is one where it used to be said the medium is the message. At one time, the media claimed to report life. Now I have the feeling that they make life, that the medium or the message becomes life. And under those circumstances, it seems to me they have a much larger responsibility than to sell papers, and that is to think about what kind of lives they are making for our children and their children.

MARIANNE MEANS: Mr. Cox, I think we do think about it. I think we do have a sense of responsibility and do think about that. I did not mean to suggest that we did not, but whom, if not government, would you have impose new standards? Whom would you have bell the cat of the press?

ARCHIBALD COX: I think the only thing we can do is to appeal to your consciences and jump on you whenever you say "it's the nature of the business."

MARIANNE MEANS: Which everyone does all the time.

THOMAS GEE: His answer is the press itself.

MARIANNE MEANS: I think we are self-monitoring. That is what we are doing here, discussing all this. What I was

---

*In 1979, the government obtained an injunction that prevented the *Progressive*, a monthly magazine, from publishing an article, based on open, unclassified documents, describing how a hydrogen bomb is made. The injunction delayed publication for six months. The government eventually decided to drop the case after other publications had printed material containing much of the same information.

wondering was if he was suggesting some other kind of mechanism?

THOMAS GEE: I do not think so at all.

DOUGLASS CATER: I think we have been too sanguine. At the risk of getting into the topic for the next panel, the question is whether this glass is half full or half empty.

I think we are moving into an age in which increased competition, the technology and all that it particularly means in electronics, is going to make it more and more difficult to even consider what are standards of proper or fair behavior in the press. The judge in the case in California—if you remember the time of the "family viewing hour" which was trumped up by the networks in an attempt to get at this question of violence and children—ruled that even the stations could not get together to impose standards on themselves.* I think that judge was a stupid judge. I think he carried so-called constitutional freedom well beyond what it can properly mean. Perhaps the family viewing hour was not the perfect formula, but certainly the effort to arrive at standards has to be done in certain concerted ways.

It seems to me the problem is visible now in prime-time network evening news—that you are getting hyped-up news programs in which entertainment value is pushing out what long-time and high-standard journalists, like Marianne Means, Harrison Salisbury, and Joe Kraft, would regard as news value.

ARTHUR GINSBURG: Who will impose those standards, Mr. Cater, in your opinion?

DOUGLASS CATER: This is the question before us. If we do not want the courts to do it and if we do not want the politicians to do it, then who does it? And I do not think we can duck that question.

---

*In 1975, Federal Communications Commission Chairman Richard E. Wiley led efforts to obtain an agreement from the television networks to avoid scheduling "programs inappropriate for viewing by a general family audience" in the early prime-time hours. The National Association of Broadcasters (NAB) adopted an amendment to its TV code designating the period between 7 and 9 p.m. as the "family viewing" time. In 1976, a federal judge ruled that the agreement violated the First Amendment, saying that the "family hour" agreement was reached primarily because of pressure from FCC Chairman Wiley, acting in response to Congressional pressures, and that the NAB, in monitoring adherence, was acting as censor. The judge said the family hour could continue, provided that broadcasters, in their independent judgment and under no government pressure, decided that it was a desirable policy.

KENNETH TOWERY: There is only one group left, and that is the people, by the choice of what they buy.

MARIANNE MEANS: But you are the people. The people must express themselves through some vehicle.

KENNETH TOWERY: They express themselves through what they buy and what they do not buy.

JOSEPH KRAFT: I do not think the marketplace is a really good cure for this disease, and I think that is the real danger. If you leave it up to the marketplace, the disease is going to get worse. It does seem to me the real cure lies in our own honesty, in our own self-consciousness, in our own intellectual responsibility.

I think Archie Cox put his finger on a very, very good point. I think we are not rising to the level of our pretensions. I think when we correct mistakes, we say that we got somebody's middle name wrong or that there was a mistake of identity. We are not intellectually honest. We are not intellectually responsible in tracing through the bad consequences of even some of our good impulses. I think that is the kind of thing we have to do for ourselves. I think we can only do it ourselves, because every cure that I know about, that I have ever heard about, even the one that I can see, I think, forming in the back of Doug Cater's mind, is worse than the disease. So it seems to me pretty imperative that there be a lot of self-scrutiny and that it be self-scrutiny at a very high level, not just the kind of thing that ombudsmen do.

DOUGLASS CATER: Well, Joe, since you can see in the back of my mind—which I am not sure I can—it seems to me that we recently had a wonderful case study of irresponsibility pushing hard against responsibility in that marathon coverage of the assassination attempt.

MARIANNE MEANS: I agree.

DOUGLASS CATER: It came out in a particular graphic image as to whether Jim Brady was dead.* Now, you would say that is a little thing, but that was an irresponsible press—and then the responsible ones have to jump to the irresponsible tune.

So if you see what's in the back of my mind, let me ask, what's in the back of your mind?

---

*On March 30, 1981, all three commercial television networks erroneously reported that Presidential Press Secretary James Brady had died of wounds received during the attempted assassination of President Reagan.

JOSEPH KRAFT: What's in the back of my mind is the same thing that is in the front of my mind. What I have been saying all along, from beginning to end, is that we have to do it ourselves, that self-scrutiny is the only answer and it has to be intense.

Maybe I did you an injustice, but I thought that what you were talking about were publishers or groups of publishers getting together through press councils and things like that and setting standards. Maybe that is not in the back of your mind. It is in the back of some people's minds, and I tend to agree with what Marianne Means said: that is not going to solve the problem, that is not a good way to do it. I just do not think it is a good practical way to do it. And if it is not in the back of your mind, I cheer.

HARRISON SALISBURY: May I say something about this? This question that we are talking about, really, is responsibility, and to a considerable extent we are talking about responsibility in the electronic media.

If we look at this in some kind of historical perspective, if we look, for example, at the newspapers in a kind of historical perspective and go back, say, seventy-five or even fifty years, you will find that the newspapers in this country were not very responsible—with a few significant exceptions. They were competing at a very low level in this marketplace that Marianne Means has talked about, and they were competing at the level that used to be called "yellow journalism"—any kind of a sensation, big headlines, anything else to sell papers. But as a result of the competitive process and of the gradual growth of standards of performance in the news field, the newspapers, by and large, began to raise their overall level of professionalism and their level of reliability, and less and less of this sensationalism crept in.

The electronic media has a rather short life history. Television has only grown up since about 1949 or thereabouts. It is learning many things that were learned earlier by the print media.

I may be too optimistic, but I do not think I am. I believe that as time goes on, it will continue to improve on this question of responsibility, the question of dedication to presenting news as a basic factor, along with a certain amount of entertainment. I am not one who says that the newspapers or the electronic media should not be entertaining. We all like to be entertained, but we want our news straight. I believe the natural processes are going to provide that, particularly if we continue to indulge in self-criticism and we get plenty of feedback from the public, and it seems to me we do get that.

EDWARD BARRETT, JR.: I agree. I think the worst thing that could happen to the press would be government control. The First Amendment used as a shield against government control, it seems to me, is its central meaning, and the press ought to hang very hard on the First Amendment as a shield. But when, dressed in the gleaming armor of Sir Galahad, the press not only has the shield up there with the First Amendment emblazoned on it, but also has the sword, and wants to use the First Amendment as a device for compelling access to governmental information, for providing all kinds of special positions for the press—I think that poses the real danger. It is that thrust which, despite the moderation of our panel, comes across very strongly, particularly as you read the professional journals of the media. The further you go in that direction, the more you make inevitable government control because, with special privileges, inevitably goes control.

One last comment: maybe there is some hope that the public will take note. Recently, I went to the faculty club for lunch. I sat down with a group of eight or ten people who, by chance, represented a pretty good cross section of the disciplines on our campus, and the discussion got around to the press and its role in the recent events. I was interested that this group was unanimous in condemning the press's role. They knew I was coming here today, and the message was, "Give 'em hell."

ARTHUR GINSBURG: I am particularly interested in the questions I raised in my introductory remarks about access, which were touched upon here, and which Professor Cox talked about. You might address yourselves a little more to that, maybe to questions of access and the constitutional problems and what will happen when the little fish swallow up the big fish—which is rapidly going on, by the way, in cable television. There are fewer and fewer voices out there, and maybe the same thing is happening in the newspapers. What are your thoughts on that?

ARCHIBALD COX: I think that if the electronic media continue to be dominated, and if the new technologies do not fragment them so that there are ample opportunities for access, and if they do not present a wider spectrum of views than they do now, we will be caught between two unpleasant alternatives: either to allow the electronic media to exclude extreme views from the political dialogue; or to develop the fairness doctrine further.

I have often thought the place where this most came to a pinch was in the total exclusion of minor candidates from the presidential debates. I am not thinking of John Anderson. I am thinking of really minor candidates. Of course, the early Republican Party would have been excluded if we had had the electronic media at that time. And I hate to see the opportunities for really novel ideas being curtailed.

THOMAS GEE: I would like to address a question to Mr. Salisbury and Ms. Means.

I must admit that I have been taken, in looking at the major electronic media, with the sameness of the presentations of the three major networks. And for that reason, Governor Connally's suggestion that they draw their bill of fare from the *Times* caught my fancy. Would you care to comment on that?

MARIANNE MEANS: Not working for the television media, I really cannot say how they make their judgments, but it is quite possible. It seems to me that what happens is that they are all trained news people. They are at the top of their profession, and they make the same judgments about what are the most newsworthy stories of the day because they are the most newsworthy stories of the day. In Washington, D.C., all the TV news comes on at the same time, so I have no way of comparing exact shows with exact shows, but when I do watch it seems to me that they do sometimes emphasize different things. They pick special segments that are different.

The real sameness comes in their judgment of what is the most newsworthy event, and I submit that it is merely consensus because it is the most newsworthy event.

THOMAS GEE: I can understand that. The same thing frequently happens with the major news magazines. You will find that they often have the same cover story. But there is more to it than that. The points of view seem to be so nondiverse.

HARRISON SALISBURY: The essence of being a trained newspaperman or journalist or a student of public opinion is the ability to evaluate the news and its importance to the world and to the country and to the community. That is one of the important things you are trained to do. So it is no coincidence, as Marianne says, that the three network news programs by and large will have much the same evaluations.

If you were to make a study of all the newspapers in the country, you would find that—let us say there are twenty stories in competition—most of those papers would have sixteen or seventeen of those stories on page one. And, if you evaluated it yourself, you would say, "Yes, those are the most important stories."

So far as viewpoint is concerned, it would be my observation that the network news programs are about as objective and almost bland, so far as editorial viewpoint is concerned, as you could find, and that is deliberately so. They have trained themselves to be objective, and I think they succeed in doing that. That doesn't mean that they aren't criticized by you or me or many other people, because often we believe that what *we* think is objective is true objectivity. And yet, as has been mentioned many times here, everyone has his or her own particular bias and his or her own particular interests. I often argue with the stories that are put on the front page of the *New York Times*. I think they leave off some stories that should have been there. I think that the coverage by Cronkite or somebody like that may show a certain bias. It probably does, but, by and large, these things blend themselves out.

I do not believe that the charge of bias, which is really what underlies this, could be proven by submission to any sort of a jury of the country.

MARIANNE MEANS: The jury would have its own bias.

JOSEPH KRAFT: I don't think it could be proven, but I think it could be advanced with a lot more information than you have put into the question. To do it, I have to sort of play ventriloquist and speak in accents that really are not mine.

Archie Cox talked about exclusion of certain voices from a presidential debate. About fifteen years ago, I think I invented the term "middle America" to describe a viewpoint that I thought was systematically excluded from the media. By the media, I mean the three networks, the national and major regional papers, and the news magazines. And I think, because of the requirements of the profession—and good requirements, because we have been improving our quality—we have been increasingly drawing our people from a narrower and narrower segment of the population. Those in the media tend to be drawn from a segment of the population that is upwardly mobile, that believes in celebrities, that tends to be, not wrongly maybe, critical of the society—which is what Governor Connally had in mind when he used the word "elitist"—that is relatively remote, increasingly remote from the working class. And I think that is a major component of bias. I think if you look at the stances we took through the sixties and the seventies—and I do not think anybody has done this very systematically—my impression is that we were the chief allies of the minority groups that came up and staked claim after claim after claim. We did it for the blacks. We did it for the young. We did it for the women. Everybody who had a bitch in this society found a friend. I am not sure that it is wrong or right, but it was not middle American and neither was it totally pluralistic. It had a real bias. That bias, I think, is still with us.

One of the sad things, I think, is that the people who bear witness against this bias are either inappropriate, like me, or else are not good at bearing witness.

EDWARD BARRETT, Jr.: I would like to pick up on that and on one of the things Archie Cox said.

In reference to access to the press, it seems to me in one sense you can say that one of the real difficulties with television, particularly, is that it makes it too easy to get access to the press. Anybody can call a demonstration. We have groups in our society who regularly get access to the press, and the media tends to feed on certain kinds of dissident groups because they make a show. If you want to get access to the press today, you don't write a letter to the editor; you get a group of people together and have a demonstration. And then the cameras will come out and you get access. In some ways, that is much too easy and it tends to distort.

ARCHIBALD COX: Well, I would comment on that—I'm afraid from the viewpoint of one who was "chief pig" in the bad years of 1968, 1970, I would add simply that it is a shame that to get on television you have to occupy a building. Perhaps that was what you were seeking to emphasize.

ARTHUR GINSBURG: Well, will there be a chance to look into that when we have sixty channels in Austin and many places have sixty or eighty channels? Will that change our view of the First Amendment and access questions? Will that in any way make the news somewhat different? Will there even be more access under those circumstances?

MARIANNE MEANS: In the sense that this is going to increase competition, it would have to change things, because competition, by its very nature, means controversy and diversity and competing factors.

ARTHUR GINSBURG: Will the media become any more responsible when they have sixty outlets and all of the news?

EDWARD BARRETT, JR.: When you fragment, you are going to fragment audiences. And in that sense, more people will find things they want to hear. I'm not sure, however, that any one individual would get exposed to any more as you fragment the audiences. He may only look at one of those sixty channels.

THOMAS GEE: Or he may become more responsible in the sense that Mr. Kraft was speaking of, because more diverse viewpoints will come across and he will not be left with the feeling that everyone on the network spends all his time talking to other people on the network.

HARRISON SALISBURY: May I comment on that, on this question of diversity, which I think is a very important and often ill-perceived fact about the criticism of the press.

When I was growing up in Minneapolis and St. Paul fifty, sixty years ago, there were in Minneapolis five daily newspapers of varying political opinions. There were three more in St. Paul. That was eight papers in the community, each one of which presented a different editorial viewpoint. Granted, most of them were solid Republican papers, but there was a gradation. They even allowed the Democrats to have one paper. The result of this was that you bought the newspaper that conformed to your own biases and your own opinion and that was an objective paper to you; the others were all lying sheets.

Today in the newspaper field, there are monopolies in most cities in the world, most cities in this country, with few exceptions. I am very familiar with this problem in New York with the *New York Times*. When the *Herald Tribune* went out of business, the *Times* willy-nilly inherited a lot of people who had been reading the *Herald Tribune*. Obviously they did not like the *Times* editorial position or they would have been taking that paper already. But now, it was the only game in town, so they became readers of the *Times* and they were not comfortable. They did not like the opinions of the *Times*. The *Times* was not solidly

Republican. It leaned to the Democratic side. It was more liberal than they liked, and it did not have any good, solid conservative columnists. They were uncomfortable and critical. They had criticized the *Times* from the outside before. Now they criticized it from the inside.

How were we to meet that problem? Well, there is no real way of meeting it, but one thing we did do on the *Times*—and I think my role was an important one—was to create the so-called "Op-Ed" page, which was a page for the presentation of opinions different from those of the *Times* and its columnists—negative opinions, oblique opinions, opposite opinions, anything which was not represented in the ordinary bill of fare. Many other papers and many electronic media today have adopted that particular solution for this specific problem. It works up to a point, but the fact remains—a fact which newspapers, I don't think, really understand—that each paper has in its total circulation a lot of people who are uncomfortable being there because the paper does not represent their particular point of view.

Whether this can be corrected by having multiple electronic channels, I just don't know. The electronic channels have not, in my opinion, developed very much in the way of varying political and economic views. They tend to follow a particular line. But this is at the root, I think, of much of the dissatisfaction and the uneasiness in the public about the press.

ARTHUR GINSBURG: I certainly do not suggest that there be a fairness doctrine for the press, which the Supreme Court rejected some time ago. But what about those people who feel uncomfortable, the middle Americans, if you will, who feel disenfranchised to some extent?

HARRISON SALISBURY: I don't think the fairness doctrine makes them any more comfortable with TV or radio.

DOUGLASS CATER: I think that the problem of having access channels which will just become ghettoes for particular groups is not really addressing the subject that we need to be coping with. I keep trying to push against the sanguine view of the future—that every day and in every way we are getting better and better. I don't see it.

I think the network news is not as high in its standards today as it was ten or twenty years ago. There are pressures for jazzing it up, for abbreviating it. And let us not just focus on news. We used to have TV documentaries that would go for some period of time. Now they have discovered that nice little format called the magazine in which, in five minutes or less, they will sum up a subject of great controversy and deliver a very pronounced decision. This is not the kind of systematic informing of public opinion that is up to the kind of challenge we face in the world today.

I agree with Governor Connally that the problems of communication are far more complex than they ever were, and I think that the instruments of communication are probably more simplistic than they were in bygone times.

JOSEPH KRAFT: I agree with you, Doug, I think. But there is one question that I really think you keep leaving around the corner, and this is a real question. The question is, What do you see that is so bad in the future, given the coming fragmentation of markets everybody believes is going to happen? What is going to be so awful about that?

DOUGLASS CATER: I think, with Dan Schorr and Ted Turner, we are going to see over time whether a cable satellite fourth network* does provide a genuine new opportunity. I am not absolutely convinced. I think it is going to be, though, an act of will and not of just natural forces. And I do think that the economics of the situation are working against it—the economics and, to a degree, the technology. We are tuning into a public that is used to thinking that if it watches thirty seconds on a complicated story, that is enough. So I would not leave the public out of this universal condemnation that I am so generously handing out.

JOSEPH KRAFT: If you are saying the problem is cultural shallowness, I agree.

MARIANNE MEANS: I'm not sure that the people, certainly not all the people who are now watching thirty seconds of an important story, would have gotten that story at all in the old days—even thirty seconds worth of it. A lot of people who are getting news and information from television—since that is what we are talking about now—would not have had the attention span or the interest to really read a long thoughtful article on that subject. The people who are interested and want to be informed and are educated will still read that long thoughtful article; the thirty seconds on television will not be enough. They are not restricted to that thirty seconds on television. They can read

---

*In June 1980, Ted Turner launched the Atlanta-based Cable News Network, a twenty-four-hour, all-news operation. CNN feeds cable systems across the country via satellite.

books or they can read articles or they can go to other sources of information.

In other words, it does not worry me.

ARTHUR GINSBURG: Basically, looking at the question of the First Amendment and whether that can survive, Mr. Cater believes that the First Amendment has been stretched beyond all limits. I would like to ask Judge Gee to comment on that aspect of it.

THOMAS GEE: I don't think there is very much doubt, from an historical point of view, that the First Amendment originally meant that the national Congress was not to make any laws providing prior restraints. That was the general intent.

Since then, it has expanded in various directions and, of course, we are all familiar with Justice Douglas's view that there can be no restraint whatever on either speech or press. And Justice Black was not far from that.

I think it is a matter of common sense. Every government has to do a certain number of things in order to govern. The nice thing about the one that we have is that there are some very nasty things that the Constitution, through the courts—not to blow our own horn—prevents people, even majorities, from doing. But really, the First Amendment is in very good health and shape right now, it seems to me. I think it is really in danger only from excesses, and it is not really in much danger from that.

We are all sitting around talking as though something bad were going to happen to the First Amendment, but nothing bad is going to happen to it unless they abolish the court system or take away our jurisdiction. But we will be the ones who are construing the law that purports to take away our jurisdiction, so you don't have to worry too much about that either.

I sometimes hear people say that the press and the courts are natural enemies. I think this is a great, great misapprehension. If it were not for the courts, we would still have the alien and sedition laws. So it is not as though the continued existence of the First Amendment were up to any voter or any speech maker. It's up to us, and it's going to continue to exist because we are going to see that it does.

KENNETH TOWERY: When you say it's up to us, do you mean it's up to you the judiciary?

THOMAS GEE: I mean it's up to the courts. That's where the rubber meets the road.

KENNETH TOWERY: I don't know that I would go that far.

Judge, how would you feel about the proposition of an official secrets act in this country?

THOMAS GEE: I don't know enough about how the British system works. I regret my ignorance. I am very scared about the idea of prior restraints on any systemetized basis.

I will say that it really devastates me to think that some person that we sent abroad, for example, in some intelligence capacity should have the rug pulled out from under him in order for somebody to sell a newspaper. But there are a lot of hard things about the way our government works. It is full of trade-offs, and sometimes you have to see something agonizing happen in order that you won't see something worse happen.

KENNETH TOWERY: Well, I think the Amendment is in good shape. I think it is going to survive, and I do not think we have to worry a whole lot about it. I have defended the press a great deal and I feel part of it, but there is one area where I do have worries: if the people ever turn away from the press in disgust, shall we say, over certain things, then I think the freedom of the press is in danger—regardless of whether the First Amendment stays there or not.

I can recall a time—and it's a matter of no great consequence now because it is all over with—when I was knocking around in these things and Nixon was getting ready to go to Moscow to talk with the leadership over there. Since it's all over with now, I guess we can talk about it. Brezhnev had an arrangement whereby he would get in his car and when he started moving, he would start talking on the phone. His calls were put through a scrambler—we had broken that code, unscrambled it, and knew what he was talking about. This was very important to us because Brezhnev was having trouble with the "hard-liners" in his country and we got information on that. This was of tremendous help to us. And there were very, very few people in the government who knew it. It was so secret that they would not even put it on paper. They would come and tell us about it.

Suddenly this information appeared in a column. It appeared in a way a normal person could not have pinpointed it, but the Soviets pinpointed it right away.

If that information had been transmitted from, shall we say, a government servant in the State Department to a Soviet agent, there would have been laws involved. But in transmitting that same information to a columnist, who wrote about it and therefore tipped off the Soviets, no laws were involved. So that is why I asked about that. And I think in that general sense, those are the things that worry me as much as anything else.

THOMAS GEE: That is very frightening. Of course it is.

EDWARD BARRETT, JR.: I would like to react for a moment to something Judge Gee said. On the one hand, we have been worrying about the press thinking it knows what is good for the world. And I think coming out of Judge Gee's comments is the implication that it is the courts that know what is good for the world.

It reminds me that I frequently tell my students, although they do not quite accept it, that the real occupational hazard of being a lawyer is that you pretty soon become convinced that lawyers and judges know what is best for the world and, therefore, we should solve all the world's problems. I have my doubts that that is the way to go.

THOMAS GEE: If we did not all think that, we would not be lawyers and judges.

DOUGLASS CATER: Just to jump on Judge Gee once more, I spent a large part of the last four years in England as vice-chairman of one of the British newspapers, the London *Observer*. Harold Evans, who is, or was, the editor of the London *Sunday Times*, I think stated the issue most succinctly in terms of press freedom there compared to here. He said that he thinks British libel law, which is much stricter than ours, has real teeth in it and the power of swift enforcement does not effectively limit the freedom of the press. In fact, on the whole, it works to the good of the press, of a responsible press. He feels that the Official Secrets Act has, by and large, not been miscarried, and the press does observe it very strictly and has to.

The one area that he criticizes, Judge, is matters *sub judice*. This means the courts can take something under advisement for years and the press is forbidden to inquire into it. So he has led a campaign against this.

THOMAS GEE: I have said a lot of things against absolutism, but it may be that there is one area in which the press ought to have an absolute right to comment without fear of being trammeled by any kind of restraint from a court. It should have the right to comment on what the courts are doing, because the courts are the ones who are undertaking—not voluntarily, but because someone asks them to—to control the press from time to time. And it seems to me that because the courts represent the only control on the press of a formal nature, probably the press ought to be able to say anything it wants to say about the courts.

I would suggest that it would bear real consideration that no injunction should ever be entered against any organ of the press. If the courts want to try to keep their secrets, let them talk to their grand jurors and their jurors and their prosecutors, but they should not tell the reporters that they cannot report what they can find out.

ARTHUR GINSBURG: Mr. Cater, you expressed the view that it may be a mistake to rely on the courts with respect to interpretation of the First Amendment. I don't know whether we are all in agreement on that position. Is it a mistake to rely on the courts? Can we depend upon the courts to protect the First Amendment?

THOMAS GEE: You don't have anybody else.

MARIANNE MEANS: We have to.

DOUGLASS CATER: I qualified that. I said "overly rely"—to use the courts as a point of first resort every time you have some feeling of abuse. The courts are human, too; they have made a lot of interpretations of the First Amendment which, read in hindsight and stretched to their limits, can be made absurd.

THOMAS GEE: Quite true. The problem here is somewhat like the one we ran into when we were talking about upgrading the press. No one can upgrade the press but the press itself. I did not intend to say that the courts were the repository of all wisdom. What I meant to say was that they are the only game in town and that the only way to get better interpretation of the law, since the courts are the ones who do interpret the law finally, is to upgrade the courts.

ARCHIBALD COX: Professor Barrett and I would claim that the professors upgrade the courts.

THOMAS GEE: Of course they do. We can use all the help we can get.

ARTHUR GINSBURG: We could probably discuss this subject and several others at great length. We did not touch upon pressures by groups such as the Moral Majority and how that affects the First Amendment. There are a number of other questions that with such a distinguished panel we could probably make a course out of here if we had the time.

But there were a number of important ideas expressed here today, including the assertions that there should be a creative tension between the press and the government; that the courts themselves are the ones to control the First Amendment; and that the press has played a major role in making democracy work.

FROM THE AUDIENCE: How do you define a free press? Specifically, do you mean absolute, unrestricted freedom under any and all circumstances? If your answer to that is no, then who is going to decide under what conditions that freedom should be limited or circumscribed?

JOSEPH KRAFT: I have no problem letting the courts decide what a free press is.

MARIANNE MEANS: No, I do not think that the privilege should be absolute. The courts have decided we should not work with malice. In the Carol Burnett case, they decided that reckless disregard of the truth demanded punishment. I agree with that. I think I would agree that there are legitimate bounds of national security. There is always a question of how to define "national security," but there are limits and I am happy to have the courts decide them.

FROM THE AUDIENCE: I agree that in the past and in the present, the First Amendment and our press has been and is pretty free. But what I worry about, after listening to Governor Connally and the future problems he foretells—energy problems, scarce resources, nuclear proliferation, economic collapse worldwide, whatever real, imagined, or perceived problems—I am wondering what the state of the press will be then? We talk about the sufferance of the press at the hands of the people, but I am worrying about the sufferance of the press at the hands of the government, if the situation is perceived to be so grave in the future.

JOSEPH KRAFT: I would like to take a shot at that because I think that is a very good question.

I think that, as you rightly inferred from some of the things that Governor Connally said, we are confronted with the coverage of increasingly difficult issues—questions such as energy shortage, pricing, large aggregates, things that happen in distant countries. For these problems the kind of instinctive tools we have as journalists really do not serve us very well. I think that poses real problems for us, because in order to cover those problems, we have to get people who are more and more expert, who are more and more trained, who are more and more equipped, who come from a narrower and narrower social base. And, inevitably, it seems to me we tend to lose touch with the country, and that, it seems to me, goes to the heart of what I think our real problem is. I think our tendency to go bananas about the First Amendment is an expression of the other problem that we really have, which is that our role is changing and we have not yet come to terms with the new role that is exceedingly demanding for us and that puts upon us demands that go well beyond just professional training in journalism school.

I think our profession is becoming increasingly difficult, and it increasingly tends to take those of us who are journalists away from ordinary Americans. We are losing touch and have to lose touch.

FROM THE AUDIENCE: I would like to direct this question to Professor Cox and to Judge Gee.

If it is true that the courts are where the rubber meets the road, do you feel that the people have a right to see more of what is going on in courts? Specifically, do you think that under the First Amendment, we have the right to see televised federal trials?

THOMAS GEE: You are asking me for a personal point of view. I can give you a personal point of view, but I am going to be somewhat roundabout.

We are supposed to have a publicly administered system of justice in this country, and from my personal point of view it seems to me that the more public it can be the better it is, so long as the means by which it is made public do not unduly interfere with the process.

That is pretty general, but I believe you can apply it specifically without much trouble.

ARCHIBALD COX: I confess that I am very conservative on the question of televising trials or even arguments.

I am worried about two things. First, I am worried about the effect upon the actors. I remember thinking at the time we were to go and argue the case of the Watergate tapes before Judge Sirica what a wonderful opportunity this would be for all the people to see how courts work and how arguments are had. Then I said to myself, well, if it were to happen, I wonder how it would affect my presentation. Would it affect it? And I had to confess to myself that it would, and it would not affect it for the better in terms of presenting the case to the judge. I really think I am about as programmed in habits of advocacy as anyone could be. Therefore, I thought that if it would affect my presentation, imagine how it would affect the pitch that was made in something like the *Bakke* case* or some other controversial case.

The other thing that worries me is the effect on a jury trial, unless the jury is sequestered. To begin with, the television stations are not going to put more than little bits of testimony on the news programs. I am very aware that the selection of those bits of testimony will say to the jurors who see the news, "Well, this was the important thing I heard today. This was the critical point in the trial." And I worry about the effect that will have on a jury's verdict. But I suppose that it is going to come about, and that I am doing some moaning and groaning on my own, worrying about the effect.

MARIANNE MEANS: Well, you must assume, though, that the jurors would have no access to the television news during the trial any more than they would have access to newspaper accounts about it. The newspaper accounts are also selective. But I don't see how it could affect the jurors. They wouldn't see it.

THOMAS GEE: I think once we get the courtrooms on the air, they are going to stay there for only a very short time. Someone once said that we would worry less about what people think of us if we realized how seldom they do.

EDWARD BARRETT, JR.: I would like to make another comment. I do not see sequestering juries as a universal panacea. I am not sure what impact that has on the fairness of the jury—to put the jury in jail for long periods of time. And that is not an easy solution.

ARCHIBALD COX: No. I did not mean to imply that it was, nor do I think the temptation to read what a witness has said in the newspaper is quite as great as the temptation to

---

*In a highly publicized case, *Regents of the University of California* v. *Allan Bakke* (483 U.S. 265, 98 S. Ct. 2733 [1978]), the Supreme Court ruled on June 28, 1978, on the issue of "affirmative action." The Court, 5-4, upheld the constitutionality of college admissions programs' giving special advantage to blacks and other minorities, but ruled that Bakke must be admitted to the medical school because the university's affirmative action program was unjustifiably biased against most white applicants. Bakke had claimed reverse discrimination because he had been denied admission to medical school, while less academically qualified minority students had been admitted.

see yourself and the witness on the evening news on television.

ARTHUR GINSBURG: There are those problems. The recent Supreme Court case dealing with the Florida law had a number of safeguards in it, and it remains to be seen where we are going to go in the federal courts on that score.*

FROM THE AUDIENCE: I would like to address my question to Judge Gee. Is the press a member of the public, and how should this affect how the courts deal with the press?

THOMAS GEE: Yes, indeed, the press certainly is a member of the public. It has all the rights of the public and all the duties.

JOSEPH KRAFT: And no special privilege at all?

THOMAS GEE: Why, of course it has special privileges. The problem is many of those privileges are shared by the public at large. They are just not often exercised.

DOUGLASS CATER: What about confidentiality of source? You would not give a citizen that privilege, would you?

THOMAS GEE: Any citizen who is willing to go to jail before he reveals his source enjoys that same privilege.

ARTHUR GINSBURG: You have a tough judge here.

FROM THE AUDIENCE: This is a question for Judge Gee. The Supreme Court said freedom of speech was limited when you yell "Fire" in a crowded theater. Now, as a judge, how would the courts know when the press is screaming "Fire" in a crowded theater?

THOMAS GEE: Well, I think I would paraphrase Potter Stewart about obscenity there and say that I can't describe it but I know it when I see it. I wish I could do better, but that is a question that would require about a two-hour answer if I got more specific.

---

*In a unanimous opinion in *Chandler and Granger* v. *Florida* (101 S. Ct. 802 [1981]), the Supreme Court, January 1981, declared that the televising of trials, even in the face of a defendant's objection, is within the bounds of the Constitution. The ruling neither endorsed nor opposed television in the courtroom, and said that Florida state courts, in allowing, under certain specified conditions, radio, television, and still photographic coverage of a criminal trial, notwithstanding defense objectives, was not on its face unconstitutional. While noting in the Court's majority opinion that "dangers lurk in this, as in most experiments," Chief Justice Warren E. Burger said these dangers do not warrant a ban on broadcast coverage. Federal courts, including the Supreme Court, make their own rules about procedures and are not obligated by this ruling, which applied to state courts. The federal court prohibition against cameras is expected to continue through Chief Justice Burger's tenure, since, as chairman of the Judicial Conference of the United States, he has a deciding voice. He has been outspoken in his opposition to television cameras in federal courts.

FROM THE AUDIENCE: My question is to Douglass Cater. What effect do you think Rupert Murdoch's* purchase of the London *Times* will have on London journalism, British journalism, and Western journalism?

DOUGLASS CATER: That is a pretty specialized question. I must say one of the questions that troubles me most now when we talk about freedom of communications is this problem of ownership. We witness the *New York Times*, for example, despite Mr. Salisbury's reservations, becoming a conglomerate owner, buying up little newspapers wherever they bob up on the market. We see this trend of big business moving into ownership of what is big enterprise and highly profitable enterprise.

Rupert Murdoch is the real buccaneer of the journalism world. We have seen what he has done in Texas, New York, and California. He's now in a very powerful position in London. I think that his acquisition of the *Times* newspapers, both the daily *Times* and the *Sunday Times*, is going to create great new problems for a free and diverse press.

FROM THE AUDIENCE: I would like to address this to anybody who cares to answer it. Do you think student publications should enjoy the protection of the First Amendment?

THOMAS GEE: Absolutely. As a matter of fact, one of the last cases that I handled before I went on the court was representation of the *Daily Texan* in a controversy of that sort. Yes.

EDWARD BARRETT, JR.: I do not think it is quite that easy, particularly where you have a student newspaper which is financed by compulsory government contributions either directly or through student fees. It is a little hard to disassociate this from government responsibility.

Also, there is a dilemma in that the editor of the *New York Times* or any other newspaper has a responsibility to his publisher. His publisher has an influence upon what he does and says. If student newspaper editors are given First Amendment freedoms with no publisher to be responsible to, that would be a fairly unique status, at least in our system.

---

*Rupert Murdoch is the Australian publisher whose U.S. properties include the *New York Post* and the San Antonio *News* and *Express*. Already the owner of two sensationalist, mass-circulation tabloid publications in Britain, Murdoch acquired the influential but financially troubled *Times* of London and the *Sunday Times* early in 1981.

THOMAS GEE: It would be unusual, and yet we are really not giving them anything. They already have it, it seems to me.

EDWARD BARRETT, JR.: I'm not sure what that comment means.

THOMAS GEE: They are citizens of the U.S. of A. running a press.

EDWARD BARRETT, JR.: If they were running the press independently of the governmental sector, yes. I don't know about the *Daily Texan*, but in most state universities, they are running the press with money that is coerced from other students, I believe, by the state.

ARCHIBALD COX: I was going to suggest that, first, the answer to the question, Does a student newspaper have the protection of the First Amendment?, is plainly yes. Then the question becomes, What is the extent of that protection? And it may be that the student newspaper has a right to publish, free of restraint by a state university. But it also may not have the right to a continued subsidy from the university if the university does not like what is published.

THOMAS GEE: Justly so.

FROM THE AUDIENCE: The American press is under fire in the Third World. You are being blamed for being biased, and I was wondering if you think it is possible for the American press to help the government in establishing better relationships with the Third World, especially now that the Third World is in danger of being engulfed by communism.

HARRISON SALISBURY: I believe in general that the press has a responsibility to bring to the attention of the public and the government, if necessary, major problems in our society or in the world society. I do not feel that the press has a specific responsibility to urge one program or another. This is an editorial responsibility which the press may take upon itself, but it is not one of the obligations of the press.

So far as the Third World problems are concerned, as in the case of any world problems, I would hope that American newspapers and the electronic media would pay attention to those serious and difficult problems, present as full coverage and interpretation as possible, and give editorial support in their editorial columns if they so desire. But the primary responsibility is to bring the problems to the attention of the public so that the public can be informed, so that the public, which is really the responsible body in this country, can bring its influence to bear on the government through its elected representatives to pursue a policy which it particularly favors.

MARIANNE MEANS: Can I add something to that? As you probably are aware, there is a move by the Third World in the United Nations—in UNESCO—to, in effect, force Western newspaper representatives to write good things about their countries.* This has been a long-running battle, and the Western press has fought it. And I agree that I consider it dangerous. It smacks too much of making us propaganda arms of the governments.

Under the UNESCO proposal, as I understand it, the Western press would be punished if it printed things that were not approved by a government. Their representatives might not be allowed in the country anymore and things of that sort. I really think that this is a threat to a free press and I disapprove.

FROM THE AUDIENCE: What role do you believe information systems, home information systems, will play in the public search for information, and will this endanger newspapers and other media?

MARIANNE MEANS: This is all so new, I am not sure how effective they will be or how much the public will pick it up or what it all entails. In general, I am for anything that expands individual access to information. The effect upon newspapers will depend on how good these home systems turn out to be and how good newspapers and TV are in response.

FROM THE AUDIENCE: We are seeing a trend in the electronic news media and, to some extent, also a trend in the newspapers, of emerging superstars. Do you feel that the people will expect these superstars to become more and more sensational in their reporting, and do you think the courts should restrain that?

---

*A number of Third World and Eastern bloc countries have supported the "New World Information Order," a subject which has been under consideration in the United Nations Educational, Scientific, and Cultural Organization (UNESCO). A variety of issues are involved in the UNESCO debate. Many Third World countries assert that the international communications system is inequitable, imbalanced, and biased against them. They object to the "dominating" role of Western news agencies and Western reporting of Third World affairs. Some are questioning the Western concept of the free flow of information. A central issue is the proper role of governments in relation to the media, and there are some basic differences over concepts of press freedom and responsibility. One proposal which has been discussed and strongly opposed by the United States and other Western nations is a proposal to "license" journalists. Other suggestions have been made for imposing

THOMAS GEE: I do not think the courts have any business enforcing notions of taste on anyone. No, sir.

FROM THE AUDIENCE: I have heard complaints that the press is becoming too influential on the thoughts of the American people. Take, for example, the American hostages. As soon as they were released, they were referred to as "heroes," when in actuality they did no heroic deed. They were simply captives.

Do you think that in this aspect, the role of the press is unconsciously changing and that it is just too influential in the lives of the American people?

JOSEPH KRAFT: I am going to give you a yes-no kind of cop-out answer on that.

One thing that I think has been running through all of our comments, and through Governor Connally's comments, that I would disagree with pretty strongly is the notion that we are decisively influential in everything we touch. We are influential insofar as the subjects we deal with do not affect the American citizen directly. The notion that we really shape public opinion, that we define and decide public opinion, is, I think, fundamentally wrong. In my opinion we tend to do it more and more in areas in which there is a choice, a kind of luxury choice between one kind of bread and another kind of bread or between this or that thing that happens in a far-off country. I think we probably are influential there.

But on things that matter to people, on things they have to pay for in blood or money, I think the American people make up their own minds on the basis of a very, very vivid experience. Those opinions become almost indestructible and have very, very little to do with editorials, op-ed pages, or even the evening news shows. But I think, increasingly, because life is in the United States perhaps less a struggle

---

external controls on the press and on international communications. The United States, while acknowledging the need for better news coverage of the Third World and for more technical assistance to Third World media and journalists, has actively resisted efforts to impose restrictions on international press freedom.

For more on this topic, see *Many Voices, One World* (Kogan Page/Unipub/ UNESCO), the 1980 report of the International Commission for the Study of Communication Problems (the MacBride Commission), which sets forth the agenda for the New World Information Order and discusses the issues involved. See also Rosemary Righter, *Whose News? Politics, the Press, and the Third World* (New York: Times Books, 1978), and "Information and Communications Issues," chapter 8 of *United States Policy and the Third World*, Policy Research Project Report Series (Austin: Lyndon B. Johnson School of Public Affairs, 1982).

for survival than it used to be, we do have a margin of tolerance for what you call luxury opinions—opinions that you can have that do not matter very much. And in that area, it does seem to me that opinion tends to be pretty dependent upon the things that come across in news. I am not sure we are as responsible about that as we ought to be, or as conscious of that as we ought to be.

FROM THE AUDIENCE: I would like to hear from both the legal people and the reporters on the issue of courts forcing the reporters to reveal their sources, subpoenaing newsroom material, which would seem to me to be one of the greatest threats to freedom of the press today.

ARCHIBALD COX: Well, I thought the *Branzburg* decision,* as a matter of constitutional law, was a sound one. I am inclined to think the press would pay a heavier price in the long run than it wanted to pay if it were given a special privilege that no one else had in this regard. There are a lot of people who would like to get access to information and give pledges of confidentiality. Professors particularly are in a category of that kind. So, I suspect, are our representatives in Congress and the state legislatures.

I am also very worried about how members of the press would use this absolute privilege. Do you really think that a reporter should be given a life or death control over the defendant in a murder case or something of that kind? I am very reluctant to trust that degree of power to any individuals or institutions, and I very much doubt whether we are cut off from much important information by the *Branzburg* rule. I know reporters often say that, but I am skeptical because it is, I think, a form of special pleading, and I am not sure whether they ask themselves, "Would I really have been unable to get that information if I had had to acknowledge that my pledge of confidentiality might have to yield to the orders of the judge?"

---

*Three 1972 Supreme Court cases relating to newspeople's privilege are collectively referred to as the *Branzburg* decision (*Branzburg* v. *Hays*, in re *Pappas*, and *U.S.* v. *Caldwell*). In its 5-4 decision, the Court, in an opinion by Justice Byron White, said, "Citizens generally are not constitutionally immune from grand jury subpoenas; and neither the First Amendment nor other constitutional provisions protects the average citizen from the disclosing to a grand jury information that he has received in confidence." The Court, in effect, ruled that reporters should receive no different treatment than average citizens. Branzburg was a Kentucky reporter who had refused to disclose confidential sources in testimony before a grand jury.

II

How Responsible Can a Free Competitive Press Be?

Opening Remarks by JODY POWELL:

Our topic is whether we believe that a free and competitive press can be responsible. I suppose I could answer that in the way that one of my Southern Baptist colleagues did when he was asked if he believed in infant baptism. He said, "Believe in it, hell. I've seen it done."

Well, I have also seen a free and competitive press be responsible. And as President Eisenhower once said about Mr. Nixon's role in foreign policy, "If you'll give me a week or two, I might think of an occasion."

Asking a former press secretary to be involved in a discussion like this about the press, particularly given the rather unfortunate course of events for me in the past few months, puts me somewhat in mind of the fellow who stood before a judge and was sentenced to be hanged and then was asked if he had any comments to make. And the fellow said, "Well, Your Honor, I know there are a lot of people in this community that think well of you, and I know there are a lot of folks that consider you a friend, and I know there may be even some people that admire you. But, Judge, to tell you the truth, you have went and ruint yourself with me."

I hope I can put my unfortunate personal experiences to one side and can at least give some appearance of objectivity as we approach this subject. The answer, it seems to me, is yes, it can, but the answer also, it seems to me, is that all too often it is not.

Responsibility may, it also seems, not be exactly the word we are looking for. We ought not, I think, to have to prove irresponsibility on the part of the press, as that term is generally understood, to be able to show that there is indeed a problem. My observation of the fourth estate has been from a very particular perspective over the past four years. My views are obviously colored by that perspective.

Insofar as the relationship I have observed most closely is concerned, that between the fourth estate and the White House, I think I should say at the beginning that, in my view, the relationship does not work very well. This is especially true if what we mean by working well is not a question of responsibility versus irresponsibility, but of whether or not that relationship works to provide a reasonable amount of accurate information to the American public so that they can make those decisions that are necessary in order to govern themselves. The reasons that it does not work, it seems to me, are more institutional than personal.

One of the more well-known columnists, when asked a question about this particular problem, offered as his analysis of the problem that the crises are getting more complex and the journalists are not. And Vic Gold* once observed that the Washington press corps stands forever poised on the brink of mental health.

But in my view, the problems in that relationship—and the problems relate to both institutions—stem much more from those institutional pressures and constraints which play upon the people in both the White House and the press. The problems are not primarily a product of malice or bias among reporters, although there is some of that, or of dishonesty and deceit within a government, although that, too, crops up every now and then. In short, I do not believe, as former Governor Maddox of my home state once said when asked about prison reform, that "the best thing to do would be to get a better class of prisoners."

I have been impressed over the past few years—watching us operate and watching those who are watching us operate operate—by the extent to which we have faced many of the same sorts of problems. Some are quite obvious. Both institutions, it seems to me, both government and the press, operate against artificially imposed deadlines, and, I might add, both are forced to deal with the deadlines of the other institution as well as their own. Both institutions routinely make decisions based upon inadequate, and oftentimes woefully inadequate, information.

Both institutions, it seems to me, continuously react to and make decisions based on rather dimly perceived expectations of what the other is doing or trying to do or about to do. Those of us in government rather continually attempt to determine where the press story is heading; and if we decide it is fifteen degrees off to the right from where we

---

*Vic Gold was Press Secretary to Vice-President Spiro Agnew and is national correspondent for the *Washingtonian* magazine.

want to go or that's where it is going to be by this afternoon, we race out to shift it back fifteen degrees to the left. And, of course, by the time we get out there, it is already twenty degrees to the left, and it ends up being thirty-five off.

People in the press do somewhat the same thing, in that they are continually trying to do two things: one, listen to what we're saying, sometimes, and then attempt to figure out what it is that we really mean by what we're saying.

It seems to me that both institutions are influenced by forces which neither is willing to fully acknowledge: politics in the case of government, money in the case of the press. Both institutions have a tendency to become overly defensive and hostile when under attack, and both institutions quite often fail to punish mistakes and incompetence sufficiently, although I think I would have to say that this may be even more of a problem in the fourth estate than in government. In government, as a more integral part of an overall system, there are those forces within the system that tend to reward and punish and to expose errors to a greater extent than occurs in the fourth estate.

That is a rather tentative list of some institutional problems that I see. As usual, listing the problems is a bit easier than describing the solutions.

Some of you may remember that during the First World War, Will Rogers gave President Wilson some advice on how to deal with the problem of German U-boats. Will Rogers said all we needed to do was to bring the Atlantic Ocean to a boil, but that he would leave to the technicians the implementation of the idea. Well, I am about to leave to the panel the question of how we go about bringing the Atlantic Ocean to a boil, but I do have one thought that I would like to toss out for some reaction.

Is there in this idea of competition a possible remedy for some of the problems that we face? I mean real competition, competition which recognizes the power of the fourth estate—and let me say parenthetically that the easiest cop-out in a discussion like this, and you hear it every now and then, is to say, "Well, we really do not have that much influence and we really are sort of at the mercy of everybody else. Therefore, our transgressions really perhaps are not quite so important." I am also talking about competition, the same sort of competition that I find both stimulating and, on the whole, constructive in politics. This is competition based upon a recognition, as I think was generally concluded by the earlier panel, that the First Amendment on the whole is in pretty good shape; that the fourth estate is not a quaking David facing day-in and day-out the threat of imminent extinction by some Goliath in the White House or in the government or somewhere else—the sort of competition, in short, that allows you to say about your adversary that he is a knave and a fool, if that be the case, and you feel you have grounds to say it.

If the *New York Times* makes a major error in its coverage of an important story, is it not possible that the reasons for that mistake might be newsworthy in the *Washington Post* or elsewhere? If ABC's coverage of an important story is basically flawed, and the public or a large segment of it is therefore misinformed, is there a fundamental reason that CBS should not devote some time to trying to find out why that happened? If a widely disseminated columnist is generally perceived to be, by those who know him best, both dishonest and maybe even a little bit touched, is that or is that not worthy of public discussion? Are possible conflicts of interest among those who describe government policy of absolutely no interest as compared to possible conflicts of interest among those who make policy?

I offer that as a point of departure. It is not a new idea nor is it the first time I have ever asked these questions. If, however, I get a good answer, that will be a first.

Panel Statements

DWIGHT TEETER, Moderator: The heavy word for our discussion seems to be "responsibility." Governor Connally asked earlier, "Is it not the responsibility of the press to defend our economic system, or, if it is not the responsibility of the press to defend our economic system, then whose responsibility is it? The press exists and prospers because of the economic system." So that is one view of responsibility.

I might also say that I did some dictionary research, looking for a good reading on what "responsibility" is, and I settled on one from Ambrose Bierce. He defined responsibility as "a detachable burden easily shifted to the shoulders of God, fate, fortune, luck, or one's neighbor."

In the days of astrology, it was customary to unload it upon a star. I remember also that there were times that two young reporters named Woodward and Bernstein were accused of irresponsibility during their Watergate coverage.

A free press—that is in the topic for this afternoon. Free by whose definition? Responsible by whose definition? I think all of us are going to profit from looking at our internal lexicons and wondering if we have our definitions right.

If it is a free press in a corporate age where more and more of the decisionmaking power for the news media seems to rest in fewer and fewer hands at a time when some very large newspaper conglomerates are complaining about AT&T's possible entry into the news business, perhaps we can, as I say, profitably look to our internal lexicons.

I know that the press is not beloved, and on occasion I quote some British doggerel that says:

You cannot hope to bribe or twist,
Praise God, the British journalist,
But seeing what unbribed he'll do,
There is really no occasion to.

I think there are a lot of people that feel that way about American journalists. But I do not think the journalists should bear the brunt of the blame either. Most certainly, the press should do a better job of reporting on the economic system, and we are struggling in that direction in our program at the University of Texas.

But, again, I am reminded of a rather sour remark by John P. Roche, who once defined American capitalism by saying, "'Every man for himself,' said the elephant, dancing among the chickens." So I guess Governor Connally would have us speak more kindly of the elephant.

PETER BRAESTRUP: Jody Powell is trying to get the lid up off Pandora's box. Imagine asking the *Washington Post* to criticize a story published in the *New York Times* and thereby risk retaliation. Newspapers are like lawyers and doctors: "Do not bad-mouth him lest he bad-mouth you tomorrow." In twenty years of newspaper experience, I wasn't even bad-mouthed by my own editors for making errors, even when they knew and I knew I had made an error.

This is not a disciplined profession in that sense. There are, I know, very few internal checks and balances partly because nobody has time, partly because once begun the process of internal discipline—finding and penalizing those who do not score 100 percent the first time—could lead to extremely difficult morale problems. This has happened in some cases since the institution of the ombudsman exercise at a number of newspapers, including the *Washington Post*, where those reporters singled out in print for criticism by their own paper felt betrayed and others in that newspaper felt that they soon would be betrayed. Such criticism no longer appears in the *Washington Post* ombudsman column.

We have to get along with each other inside, and the best way to get along with each other inside in a chaotic situation is not to make too many waves. There are papers where there is internal discipline—I think particularly of the *Wall Street Journal*, and when I worked on the *New York Times*, in the Washington bureau, James Reston and his deputy, Wallace Carroll, were quite good nitpickers. But nitpicking has disappeared—the old grouch with the green eyeshade who questioned the assumptions; even the issue of the reporter's sources has become an anachronism.

The *New York Times*, long after the fact or well after the fact, would criticize (but not by name) those errors, grammatical and otherwise, in a marvelous newsletter put out by the late Theodore Bernstein as assistant managing editor. There was no pain. There was no stick. Some editors fear that they will inhibit the reporter's élan, his eagerness to grab a good story, if they insist on too much second thinking, too much reflection. A person can bat .500 in the newspaper business, and if he hits a couple over the wall all is forgiven. We have the case of a prominent reporter who has just, seven years after the fact, published a recantation of what amounted to an extended smear of a career U.S. diplomat allegedly involved, but not actually involved, in the Allende situation.* That reporter will suffer no harm as

---

*On February 9, 1981, the *New York Times* printed a page-one article headed: "New Evidence Backs Ex-Envoy on His Role in Chile." The article by Seymour M. Hersh said: "For six years Edward M. Korry, U.S. Ambassador to Chile from 1967 to 1971, has insisted that he was not involved in and indeed tried to stop White House efforts to induce a military coup in Chile in 1970 to prevent Dr. Salvador Allende Gossens, a Marxist, from assuming the presidency.

"Evidence has come to light suggesting that Mr. Korry, despite his strong opposition to the Allende candidacy, was frozen out of the planning for a proposed military coup and warned the White House that it would be risking another 'Bay of Pigs' if it got involved in military plots to stop Dr. Allende's election.

"Mr. Korry has not worked in his professions, journalism or public affairs, since 1974, two years after columnist Jack Anderson published International Telephone and Telegraph Corporation documents that seemingly linked Mr. Korry to joint

far as we know. He missed one. He got it wrong. The fact that an individual has severely suffered, et cetera, et cetera, is really not the subject of tears in the newspaper business.

So we do not have that kind of tough internal discipline, except by individual editors here and there.

A second trend is taking place in the business as a whole. (We are very trendy.) If the problem in the print media is one of shrinking diversity, referred to earlier by Harrison Salisbury and others, the problem on the television side is perhaps one of a shrinking seriousness. We have a new generation coming on who are not veterans of print. Dan Rather does not even pretend to call himself the managing editor, as Uncle Walter did, of the CBS Evening News.

TV news, as ABC producer Av Westin put it, is a branch of show business. Its values are essentially those of the extreme spectrum of the old print media: melodrama, pathos, crying refugees, shouting Iranians, the lot. As Doug Kiker of NBC News put it, "We're all making little Hollywood movies."

There is a ratings competition in TV which does not exist in print. There's a fundamental economic difference involved. We cannot bore the viewer. We play it safe. We supply meaning, theme, and context to often incomprehensible film through having a script read on camera with seeming authority by a reporter, who is doing what is called the stand-upper. So the result is a kind of a very highly packaged entertainment package vying for ratings with other entertainment packages known as network news shows. Inside the industry, these news shows are viewed in

---

I.T.T.-Central Intelligence Agency operations to block Dr. Allende's election.

"Mr. Korry expressed particular bitterness toward the *New York Times* for what he said was unfair reporting about his role in articles in 1974 that revealed the C.I.A.'s activities in Chile and in refusing in later years to investigate his actions accurately.

"Mr. Korry ... insists that his sullied reputation and his early inability to get appropriate work stem from publication of the I.T.T. documents and from two subsequent widely publicized investigations by Senate committees.

"Much of the new evidence, including highly classified internal C.I.A. documents, was provided by a former intelligence official...."

In a February 22, 1981, letter to the editor of the *Times*, Korry wrote that the article "finally ends a personal nightmare of nine years' duration. That nightmare started in 1972 with the publication by Jack Anderson of the so-called I.T.T. papers, whose egregious and malicious authors attributed to me White House orders which, as your paper now acknowledges, were unknown to me then, as later...."

(See also, U.S., Congress, Senate, *Hearings before the Select Committee to Study Governmental Operations with Respect to Intelligence Activities of the United States Senate*, 94th Cong., 1st sess., vol. 7, "Covert Action," December 4-5, 1975.)

economic terms just as other shows, like "Dallas" and "Lou Grant," are viewed—in terms of their ratings.

HODDING CARTER: I came out of a far different world from the one described earlier by Joe Kraft, and, to a large degree, accurately described by Jody Powell. That is to say I came out of the world of personal journalism, of vicious and continuing attacks by newspapermen against newspapermen in what I still fondly remember as the best old days of all, in which newspaper editors cared enough about their ideas to attack the character of newspaper editors who didn't share them and to reveal as vigorously as possible the sins and transgressions of the lousy liberal, the dirty integrationist, or the conservative "seg," whatever it might have been. We went at each other with great vigor and for a long time in Mississippi, as in fact you did here in Texas.

Something funny happened on the way to the store, and that is we decided that we were really members of a rather fashionable men's club. You know the kind I'm talking about. You sit around, you talk in hushed terms, you're surrounded by fine leather chairs, and you wouldn't think of criticizing a fellow member to his face or raising unpleasant issues about each other's behavior within the confines of the club. And the membership of the club is getting smaller and smaller all the time. The number of possible critics in real terms, which is to say ownership, is getting smaller, and the willingness to indulge in the vice of self-criticism is virtually nonexistent.

I write an occasional column for the *Wall Street Journal*. I commend the *Journal* to you for a different reason than Peter Braestrup did. I disagree almost totally with the editorial policy. I agree totally with its practice of assaulting the *Times* and the *Washington Post* from time to time for their editorial biases, mistakes, or what have you. It is refreshing, a refreshing bit of sunshine in a very stuffy world.

The topic, however, is not about this stuffy club in itself but about the question of responsibility in a free, competitive press, and there the club problem begins to enter in.

I disagree with Joe Kraft on something else as well. The institution of the press is increasingly a big business institution, fulfilling the nightmare of old Joe Patterson,* who,

---

*Joseph Medill Patterson, member of a prominent newspaper publishing family, founded the New York *Daily News* in 1919. Within five years, the *News*, with its sensationalist tabloid style, had the largest circulation of any New York paper.

somewhere along the line in the creation of the *Daily News*, remarked that there was a cycle to newspapers in which the owners came from the people, reflected the people's needs and concerns, grew prosperous doing it, forgot their earlier concerns, and their publications became corrupt and finally divorced from the reality of those people. That has happened to a lot of newspapers. It has happened to the newspaper business.

It is instructive that where there were once eight newspapers in the Twin Cities of St. Paul and Minneapolis, there are now not even eight newspapers in the twin political and communications capitals of this nation, Washington and New York. The people who run the enterprises now are big power people. They are separate from the public—"they" being not the reporters so much as the owners. They increasingly represent not the communities in which they operate, but a megacommunity simply divorced from the knowledge, the concerns, even the economic conditions of most of the people they serve.

So I say to you it is not that the press has been the handmaiden over the last twenty years of every social revolution that has come along. The press hasn't gotten ahead of a single wave in twenty years. The press has not seen one of them coming. The press in fact had to be kicked in the face with each one, repeatedly, growing out of the people in their own communities, before they discovered it.

We have suddenly discovered the realities of our own communities again and again.

I'll never forget when the *New York Times* began a survey of the problems in Harlem in 1962 or 1961, and the lead was something like: "In recent years, the Negroes of Harlem have become unhappy with their condition." And I'm not being facetious here. It was roughly that.

We are terrified of being called irresponsible. We have become so stuffy that the one sin we don't want put to us is irresponsibility—if that word is uttered by the other members of the club or by those who inhabit the same economic plateau as our own. If others call us irresponsible, we take it as a badge of honor.

Let me just conclude it with this: for me, the answer to the problems of irresponsibility in press performance is, in fact, more competition, more freedom, more press, more diversity. And the one question that was shied away from in the first panel, and that we are going to shy away from here, and that you have to find an answer to—if we're going to meet the problem, which is a real disaffection between the people and the press—is, How are you going to reverse the trend toward fewer and fewer controlling more and more in this most vital of institutions, communications?

GEORGE CHRISTIAN: I can look back on my years in public life and as a private citizen, and I find many instances in which I believed I was sinned against by the press. I can also recall the period when I was a wire-service reporter and identify times when I sinned against others. I have been in government. I have been in the press. I am in private business. So from this mixed bag of innocence and guilt, I submit a few observations. Some of them will track what Hodding Carter just said.

First, the press is the only one of our great national institutions with an objective that is essentially negative. Government, for example, is structured to deal with problems and solutions. The press focuses on blemishes and imperfections. By its nature, it's constantly picking over the bones, looking for mistakes. So it fulfills a useful, if sometimes morbid, purpose in our society.

Second, the First Amendment can be interpreted as a license for irresponsibility. It allows each element of the news media to pretty well establish its own rules. And beyond that, to a great extent, it allows each reporter and editor to establish individual rules.

I submit, therefore, the remarkable evidence, to me, that most of those in the media have chosen to be responsible in at least equal measure to those in government, business, labor, and the learned professions.

Third, many people in public life would prefer to function out of the press's line of vision, except at those times they desire to manipulate the press. We should keep in mind that much of the news, as it relates to government, is based upon a system of leaks, counterleaks, gossip, whispers, and intentional manipulation of the press. What comes out of the typewriter of an enterprising reporter frequently is the result of information laid before his eyes or spoken into his ear by an enterprising public servant with his own special ax to grind.

Fourth, we are beyond the point in time when a public official or anyone else, no matter his station in life, can state a simple fact and have it believed without serious question. This is indeed the age of incredulity.

Fifth and finally, when we worry about the excesses of the press, perhaps we should give the excesses of government at least equal billing. I suggest that the steady stream of scandalous events involving our leaders sets a poorer example for our children than irresponsible actions of the free press. I suggest also that the excesses of many government agencies and regulators, well known to any citizen unfortunate enough to face bureaucratic arrogance and obstinance, are far more injurious to our democratic system than the mistakes and prejudices of the news media.

In our democracy, which is still strong despite its imperfections, the competitive press can do great damage to individuals and to causes, and often does. But I would be more concerned if the press became less competitive than it is.

I want the three networks and the myriad of cable outlets which are just arriving on the scene to fight hard for viewer attention, and I believe this is going to solve part of the problem that Hodding Carter referred to. I want the mighty *Los Angeles Times*, Tony Day, to be taunted by the *Los Angeles Herald Examiner*.

ANTHONY DAY: We are.

GEORGE CHRISTIAN: I say that because I need to have full employment for my family, and I have a daughter on each paper.

Our danger, it seems to me, lies not in the competitive nature of the media, but in the possibility of concentrated media power. I am hopeful that the courts will impede this concentration through proper application of the antitrust laws. I assume that the public airways will continue to be doled out to free-enterprise broadcasters with competition in mind. In the meantime, it doesn't bother me at all that in our society, which is becoming ever more structured, there is at least one loose wheel rolling around, bumping into things, and keeping us on our toes.

ANTHONY DAY: I would like to turn around this question we have. Instead of, How responsible can a free competitive press be?, I really think it ought to be asked, How irresponsible dare a free competitive press be, particularly when newspapers and large combinations of newspapers are faced with the kind of threat of government intervention that they fear and that George Christian apparently would like to see?

The point is that I think sometimes the press, in order to fill its obligations to itself and its readers, has to run the risk of appearing to be absolutely irresponsible. Being responsible too often means following conventional wisdom or prevailing opinion or listening to strong and powerful government claims.

Twenty years ago, the press, vis-à-vis the United States Government, was pretty tame, and yet there was delivered a speech that was the most powerful and serious claim to press self-restraint that I know of in the post-war years. The speaker said that the United States was faced by a monolithic and ruthless conspiracy that relied primarily on covert means of expanding its sphere of influence. And this conspiracy put the United States in a situation of peace and peril which knows no precedent in history. He said that every newspaper now asks itself, "Is it news?" "All I suggest," he said, "is that you add the question, 'Is it in the interest of national security?'" He called for far greater public information but also far greater official secrecy. He asked for specific new steps or machinery for a voluntary system of press restraint.

The speaker was President Kennedy in April 1961, after the Bay of Pigs, and he was disturbed by the press account that had come out in advance about the Bay of Pigs. Actually, what had happened was that the President had already seen a kind of voluntary press restraint. Various publications had gotten wind of the invasion and the President had persuaded those publications to tone down their coverage.

Had they published everything they knew and had they hinted at everything they suspected about American involvement in the Bay of Pigs, the American people, I think, and certainly the American newspaper industry in general would have condemned them as being absolutely irresponsible.

As it turned out, the President later changed his mind and came to think that had more been published, less would have been done by the United States, and national security in the end would have been better off.

But my point here is that what is truly responsible is not always respectable. Someone mentioned earlier this morning Harrison Salisbury's trip to Hanoi. Harrison was recommended by the Pulitzer Prizes panel for a prize for those articles about Hanoi, but the jury was overturned by the Pulitzer Advisory Board—this was in 1967—on the grounds that his trip was against the national interest. Indeed, one member of the advisory board, I am reliably told, called the articles treasonous.

My point here is that what is commonly thought to be responsible is not always responsible.

Several years ago, *Ramparts* magazine, a no-count, low-down magazine, published a lot of material about the CIA which respectable opinion in my business scoffed at. Most of it has turned out to be true. A generation ago, Hodding Carter's father took on the very "irresponsible" and unrespectable job of challenging the established authority and the established powers in Mississippi. We honor him now. Those of us outside of Mississippi honored him then, but what he did isn't always the easy or the popular thing to do.

What I'm suggesting is that we should watch out for this word "responsibility." It can be a trap. We have to make sure that it doesn't turn out to be a synonym for "conventionality."

MARK McKINNON: Like Mr. Day, I think we're confronting the structural problem inherent in the question. And unlike some of the other panelists, I think I have a degree of optimism about all this.

The problem in the question, I think, is that it implies an inherent incongruity between a free competitive press and a responsible press. If you can't discuss responsibility in absolute terms and have to measure it in degree, then that perhaps is a fate we have to accept. The only alternative to a free competitive press, given those guidelines, would be something incompatible with democratic ideals and prone to gross distortion of fact. I think such a press society might be one resembling the one Mr. Connally spoke of earlier, one that would not be critical and negative. Such a society might report as fact that John Lennon killed himself with drugs, rather than that he was murdered. In such a society, "responsibility" would mean being accountable only to oneself and not to the public. So it would be absolute in those terms, but, of course, that wouldn't be acceptable.

So we can see that the system has a congenital flaw, yet agree that it really is worthy of protecting and keeping around. The problem becomes not how to cure the disease, but rather how to keep the condition from degenerating into a terminal state.

Again like Mr. Day, I think the question in reality becomes, How irresponsible can a free competitive press be and still survive or be worth saving?

The press isn't on trial to defend itself. I think we would all agree with George Bernard Shaw that the press is an institution which is unable, seemingly, to discriminate between a bicycle accident and the collapse of civilization. I think it would be perjury to deny guilt or claim summary innocence. The press volunteers that transgressions are committed occasionally but that it generally does so only in order to expose a greater crime and to preserve a greater justice. So I think our judgment of those transgressions has to be tempered by what the motive is—whether it is in self interest or the public interest.

The issue of responsibility emerges when the cost of stalking the prey exceeds the reward of the bounty. So I prefer the absolute terms, really. I think that a free competitive press can be responsible. But that's contingent on one thing. I think it's contingent on our institutions of higher education. I think people in our society have come to recognize the truth and seek the truth and will seek those publications which print the truth. I also think it's appropriate that this symposium is being conducted in this academic environment because the institutions of higher education have to accept a responsibility to provide the tools to those people who will be the journalists of tomorrow. I think we all agree that in our society today things have gotten so complex that we're dealing not just with surface issues anymore, we're dealing with complex economics, complex international problems. Therefore, what the institutions must accept is a responsibility to provide not just a specialized program but a broad education in philosophy, the sciences, literature. What is happening is that they are teaching people how to write and, no matter how well we write—we can be equipped with complete sentences and jump dangling participles—unless we're equipped with the ability to think we will never discover the truth because we'll never ask the right questions.

I'll close by quoting the namesake of this building,*

---

*The Lyndon Baines Johnson Library.

"Where liberty has arisen, learning must be cherished or liberty itself becomes a fragile thing."

HERBERT SCHMERTZ: Probably only in Texas would they feel obligated to bring an oil man into this august group.

I'm not sure that my perspective is all that different. As a matter of fact, I am going to change my name to "A" next time so I can go ahead of Peter Braestrup because Peter covered a great deal of what I wanted to talk about. But I'm going to try to add a little bit to what he said.

About a week or ten days after Dan Rather replaced Walter Cronkite, I was out with some CBS newspeople and I said, "How do you think Dan Rather is doing?" And the CBS newspeople said, "Oh, terrific. 26-20-20." I said, "Is this some new code?" He said, "No. The ratings: Rather 26, ABC and NBC 20-20. He's doing great." I said, "Well, yeah, but I mean aren't you going to tell me about his journalistic thing?" They said, "Well, he's got the new background. They changed the blue. He looks great. He looks terrific. He got a haircut. It's going very well."

You know, if that wasn't a tipoff that they were in the entertainment business, I'm not sure what might be.

I did want to take issue, though, with something Peter said. He said he thought it was a basically economic drive that caused them to adopt entertainment standards and values in their drive for audience. It clearly is a drive for audience and they clearly do use entertainment values to get that audience. But I'm not sure that the motivation is particularly economic. My experience has been that there is almost a Super Bowl locker-room, machismo kind of environment that surrounds the networks—that is if they're not number one somehow their manhood is in question. And it's not necessarily economic.

The print media are pretty quick to wash their hands of the whole problem. But I would submit to you that print bears some of the blame for that problem. The gossip columns in print continuously write about the anchorpersons on television. They continuously write about who is number one. They continually foster this Super-Bowl-mentality kind of thing, that so-and-so is up and so-and-so is down. It is all pure gossip. There are very few people who are really interested in that outside of a few people who hang around the bar at age twenty-one. But somehow the people who are interested in it tend to run the networks.

We now have a structure where the network news' objectives and the tests of success or failure are tests of the entertainment business.

The anchormen are superstars. They are paid performers' salaries, not journalists' salaries. The content is determined by the film editors and producers, who are faceless, nameless people, but they are directed and trained to get that twenty-second bite that is going to hold audiences. That's the test—to entertain, not necessarily to inform.

Interviews—how many times have those of you who have been interviewed been told by a television reporter, "Keep it short or we can't use it"? The material must be visually exciting and emotional, not necessarily informative.

These procedures inhibit the serious, responsible journalist who wants to work in television. I once thought of getting buttons printed that said, "Free the Television Journalist." Television journalism cannot handle or will not handle "talking heads."

Can you imagine what would happen to the politician if he came out of an important meeting and he was asked a question and he said, "I'd like to go home and think about that overnight and let you know tomorrow." Imagine what television would do to him. It would be a disgrace. If Hodding Carter, when he was at the State Department, had said, "I'd like to think about that one," they would have made a fool out of him on television.

DANIEL SCHORR: He did and they did.

HERBERT SCHMERTZ: Somehow, one of the myths that has developed is that "60 Minutes" is a serious piece of journalism. "60 Minutes" is pop journalism. It's entertainment. If it were in print, it wouldn't be taken seriously, I don't think.

Now, is all that necessarily bad, good, or indifferent? Is it causing any problems? If it's not causing problems, why are we wasting our time even discussing it or criticizing it?

In the industries in which I have been involved, my experience has been, for example, that we make nuclear power policy in this country based on demonstrations, not on any informative debate. We make defense and foreign policy decisions based on demonstrations. We make economic and tax policy based on TV reports of thirty seconds in duration about meaningless quarter-to-quarter profits increases or decreases. The result is—I have only cited a few examples, and I'm sure all of you can think of others—that congressional leaders, politicians, executive branch people are making policy based on what they think the public is perceiving when it gets the evening news. I have had innumerable Congressmen say to me, "I know you're correct in what you're saying, but I can't handle it with my constituents. You get on the evening news and convince my constituents that you're correct and then you come back and talk to me."

Well, that's another story—getting on the evening news. They won't place controversial issues of public importance in paid spots, and it's very difficult to get any time unless you're willing to go out and demonstrate. I seriously thought of organizing a businessman's march on Washington in which we would burn all the forms we have to file with every government agency. We would have a twenty-four-hour vigil in front of the Federal Trade Commission. We would get on television.

But that's not the way policy ought to be made, in my opinion. It ought to be made based on rational debate and rational flow of information.

To sum up, how could television news improve? First of all, I think that they clearly should expand the amount of time available so that journalists could develop a story rather than have to live with the twenty-five-second bite. They should allow participants to speak longer and more directly, the way the MacNeil-Lehrer show does. They should encourage freelance journalism. In network television, the tradition of freelance journalism virtually doesn't exist.

They should allow op-ed presentations on television network news. They should take letters to the editor. Can you imagine—a journalistic entity like the evening news takes no letters to the editor? All newspapers take letters to the editor.

This has been covered by Jody Powell and others, but I did make a note. The press should cover the press as a business and an institution. It should report on its errors and omissions. We get no reporting of that sort whatsoever.

And lastly, the issue dear to my heart, they should take paid issue advertising by those with a point of view. If that point of view is ridiculous, those ads will not be taken seriously. If they're not ridiculous, all they can do is add to the spectrum of views and opinions and increase the debate and lead to more rational judgments.

The last suggestion I would make is that we ought to look at the British experience. In Britain, several different corporate broadcasting entities have access to the same channel at different times during the week. We could increase diversity on the networks if we let different corporate entities or other entities have access to one channel at different times during the week. London Weekend, for example, has the commercial channel on weekends and other companies have access to it at different times. That could lead to diversity. There's nothing written anywhere that says one company has to have a certain channel twenty-four hours a day, seven days a week.

DANIEL SCHORR: The temptation is strong to comment irresponsibly on almost everything that has been said so far, right up to and including the remarks of Jody Powell on the shaky mental health of reporters, which I listened to, knowing his own striking contributions to that.

But in my years working on the Cronkite show, I learned that in three minutes you can make only one point at best and sometimes not that.

There is one point above all other points I want to make, so I will waive discussion of all the other statements made earlier, some of which I agree with more, some less, and some not at all.

The First Amendment is in trouble today because the industry that the First Amendment was created to protect has grown far beyond the bounds of what it was meant to protect. It is being stretched now to protect not simply the gadflies of John Peter Zenger, pamphleteers and so on, but to protect a giant industry. It was written to make it possible for journalists without the interference of Congress to serve as gadflies against the government establishment. It has become today a vast establishment of its own.

It would be idle to overlook the fact that there is suspicion, reservation, worry, concern, and hostility among people in America today about what is no longer called the press, which was good, but about the news media, which is somehow bad, because it includes television. That was demonstrated here even in the title of this symposium, along with the remarks that were made and pervaded almost all the questions that were asked from the floor. People feel they are being force-fed, that they are being given diets of violence and sex for ratings points and millions of dollars, that the news is somehow manipulated. They fear that they are losing control of themselves, their lives, what they think—that they are being brainwashed. It is a pervasive impression, and if somebody doesn't realize that that impression exists then we will not save the First Amendment.

I would submit to you, however, that while the target may be right, the ammunition is wrong. There has been a great deal of discussion about journalists-elitists, what they do and how they do things. The fact of the matter is that journalists today in the news media, so-called, have become less and less relevant to the important things that happen.

The news media today are like a whore, an easy pushover for anybody who knows how to manipulate them, starting with the President of the United States. The world of news today is largely a photo opportunity; that is, generated. The world of news today is Barbara Walters begging Jody Powell for an exclusive interview with President Carter and maybe getting it if it suits him. The world of news today is supplication—being led around to where a candidate or a President will stand in front of a factory, where he is, not to look for votes, but just to look for a photographic background which will be fed back in time for the evening news. And we're all suckers because we have to be, because we're competing with each other.

Those who can command television as easily as those in power can, do it. But what of those who can't? What of those who know that the only way to achieve identity, be it for a cause or for a person or for a campaign or candidacy or whatever, is to be seen on "that God-damned tube"? They learn their own ways.

The one statement that I explicitly disagree with is that newspeople in television tend to identify themselves with minority causes. They do not. But their attention can be commanded to minority causes. If you can't get television's attention by saying something peaceful, as Martin Luther King did, then you'll get the attention of television by saying something more menacing, as Rap Brown and others did, because it makes good footage on the evening news and scares the daylights out of people and helps to increase the ratings. And all of those who haven't learned how to get on television peaceably very soon learn how to get on it forceably. In the end, we end up with terrorism in which the object in many cases is the hijacking of television.

You are right to be concerned today about television as a force and a power and a phenomenon in our society. You are wrong, however, if you think that journalists have much to do with it. The journalists are more sinned against than sinning. They are more manipulated than manipulative. And some of the people who sit here and criticize the press have been some of the most successful manipulators of the news media.

If the First Amendment is to be saved, if the question has to be addressed now about a free and competitive press, it will be by every journalist every morning getting up and saying, "I will do what I can to resist manipulation. For every photo opportunity, I will try to explain why that photo opportunity is created. For every time something is put before me, I will have to use it because it's a part of what I have to use. I will also try to find out what they aren't showing me. I will try to go beyond it. I will try to explain it. I will try to expose all the process." And if there is to be a new dedication to the First Amendment today, it should be to fight the way television has been capitulating to manipulation by those who know how to do it.

JODY POWELL: Let me say, first of all, with regard to the comment about successful manipulators being critical of the press, I'm obviously exempt from that inasmuch as if I had been that successful I wouldn't even be here.

I think we may, in what Dan Schorr said, hopefully be about to join an issue here. It has always seemed to me that too often when we attempt to go at particular problems in the fourth estate, the defense is a very eloquent and meaningful and important statement about the problems that the institution faces. And manipulation is certainly a problem. We in government certainly do try to manipulate it—with much less success, let me say, than is generally accepted. But, having identified that problem and the need to be wary of it, or, as Tony Day said, the problems of being too conventional, of being afraid to take chances, it does not seem to me that that goes to the question of what we should do about those problems, those inequities, those mistakes that do exist. Or are we saying, in fact, that the dangers of conventionality are so great and the dangers of manipulation are so great—that they are so overpowering and threatening—that we just shouldn't worry about our transgressions for fear that in attempting to deal with them, we will fall into the much greater trap?

I was struck a little bit by the comment that the transgressions of the press tend to be—and I think I've got this quote about right—tend to be for the most part in the pursuit of a higher good. Well, if you want to know one clear difference between the fourth estate and the government, I can, by God, imagine what would have happened to me if I had stood at the podium in the White House and said, "Well, most of our transgressions tend to be in pursuit of a higher good." That would not have flown even so far as the first row of seats.

I guess overall—and I'll make this final comment and hush on this point—one of the biggest mistakes on the part of the fourth estate is to feel on occasion that those who have criticisms to make, those who object strongly sometimes, perhaps with rhetorical excess, to the way you do your business are really out to do you in. A lot of those people—and I hope I include myself in the group—do not want to see you done in, certainly not in the next four years. We want you around, but we also want to let you know some of our concerns and some places where the skin is still a little raw and see if we can't try to keep some of those things from happening to other folks.

Panel Discussion

ANTHONY DAY: I want to say a word in behalf not of newspapers but of the evening news. None of our brothers from the commercial networks is here, and I wonder if just a little bit too much isn't being asked of the evening news.

Walter Cronkite, when he used to go around making speeches, would point out that fewer words are spoken in his half-hour show than there are on page two of our newspaper, which is a compilation of one-paragraph news briefs. Cronkite pointed out constantly that that was a limitation. It is a limitation. After all, all the person on the evening news is doing is reading what in a sense amounts to a précis of the Associated Press budget briefs on the wire and showing you a few pictures. If you expect more in a half hour you shouldn't; it is not possible within the limitations of the human voice and the human eye. You have to go to the newspapers to get more. Don't ask more of Chancellor and Rather and Reynolds than they can possibly deliver. What they do, they do very well. They give you an intimate sense of the scene, a quick flash. They can give you a sense of character. It is not quite real. It is certainly not analysis. It is certainly not background. It is sometimes distorted, but it is presented in a way that newspapers simply can't duplicate.

That's about as far as I think I want to go in defense of TV.

HODDING CARTER: When I was listening to Dan Schorr, I was thinking for a moment before he fully developed his thought that he was talking about the poor little match girl. You know, poor little match girl, standing out there on the street corner with all these big forces out there busily running over her, running around her, and she is practically incapable of doing anything—she must accept the manipulation. And then, of course, he tied it off and that wasn't what he was saying after all. He was just saying that that's *almost* the way it is. And occasionally, some good reporters, when they get up in the morning, remind themselves that they have a larger obligation.

I didn't agree with a heck of a lot of what Governor Connally said this morning, but one thing he said is an absolute reality. This is a very big business with very big resources capable of doing four times as much as it's doing now in the provision of basic news to you and still making a good profit. Ask any one of these enterprises to measure their profit margin against that of an oil company, and you begin to see something you can call obscene, and it ain't the oil company.

HERBERT SCHMERTZ: I've seen large profits, but I've never seen an obscene one.

HODDING CARTER: I was only using the old editorial line about the oil company here.

But I once debated a major network's vice-president for news who explained to me at some length why they couldn't do a better job in network news. He said only two out of the three news operations are making money now. If a newspaper made that argument, if it said, "We haven't quite filled up the whole newspaper with ads yet, so we can't do a good job of news," you'd run the First Amendment out of the country.

Well, the fact is, all of the resources are there to do five times as good a job as the newspapers and television are doing.

I want you to look at the serious newspapers.

Does somebody have a newspaper?

I think sometimes we're talking about some mythical beast. Begin at the back of the paper and bring it forward and exclude the *Wall Street Journal*. Take the 35 percent which is devoted to news, then take out of it what goes in the news hole, the comics, the horoscopes, take out the sports, take out the happy-talk news and the gossip, take out the women's section or the style section or whatever they call it these days, and you suddenly get down to that part of the news which either offends or attracts you or has some impact on you. And it will come down to being maybe 10 percent of that paper. And then you remember only that aspect of that 10 percent which is grotesque or which is in one way or another frustrating or brutal, because that's what we remember.

But the fact is most of that product is filled up with stuff which, under some definitions, may be serious and thoughtful and insightful, but it used to be called froth and trash and gossip. Now it inhabits a great portion of a steadily declining news hole of every newspaper.

Now, we have the resources—and I still say "we." It's my business. We can do a lot better, and it's not the courts that stand between us and the First Amendment. It's just ourselves and our own performance. We are the final defenders of it and we can do a lot better by simply doing a better job of relating to the needs of the people we supposedly serve.

PETER BRAESTRUP: I think we've been laboring a little heavily on the brethren. A lot of this discussion never took place fifteen years ago, and it took a different form ten years ago. Ten years ago, Vice-President Agnew was talking about a liberal conspiracy.* The problem, of course, was much

---

*Vice-President Spiro Agnew made a series of statements and speeches highly critical of the media. Much of his criticism was contained in two controversial speeches: one in Des Moines, Iowa, November 3, 1969, and one in Montgomery, Alabama, November 20, 1969. The first aimed at the television networks, while the second focused on the print media. Agnew concluded his second speech with these comments: "When they go beyond fair comment and criticism they will be called upon to defend their statements and their positions just as we must defend ours. And when their criticism becomes excessive or unjust, we shall invite them down from their ivory towers to enjoy the rough and tumble of public debate. I do not seek to intimidate the press, the networks, or anyone else from speaking out. But the time for blind acceptance of their opinions is past. And the time for naive belief in their neutrality is gone."

more serious than a conspiracy, as you have learned.

But one of the problems, I think a generic problem, that a lot of people do not realize is that newspaper editors and managers are not intellectuals. In very few cases is there a coherent world view. This is lamented by academics. It probably is a good thing. It makes the newspaper people, in Washington in particular, extremely dependent—and again, I refer particularly to Washington—on coherence and, to some degree, on trust in the federal government and the President and his people.

Newspaper reporters do not know very much on a given day about what's really going on in the government. It is impossible. It is too complicated. But they have a good sense of smell. So when things are going badly or there is a sense of incoherence, a sense of lack of direction, a sense of inconsistency in policy and action, or simply a lack of action or lack of reaction to a crisis, the press tends to smell this instinctively, like a dog senses when you fear him. And they tend, when the President in particular does not take a strong line, does not appear to be up front and exerting consistent and coherent leadership, to be lost. A vacuum is created, and they go elsewhere.

If the President can't be coherent, consistent, firm, reactive, the press is lost. It has no framework within which to deal with whatever the crisis is. This occurred repeatedly during the Vietnam War. When the President, whether President Nixon or President Johnson, appeared to be taking charge of things in a crisis, there was very little panic in the press. When either one of them did not take charge, the result was a kind of compounding of the panic. The press in Washington reacts like Wall Street to bad news. The President has to get on top or appear to be on top of the situation. When he does not seem to be on top of it, the press goes bananas.

I think what some of these extreme cases illustrate is the dependence of the press on a frame of reference, on an agenda, on the President and his people. It explains in part why the press was so slow to pick up something like the civil rights movement or the women's movement or the candidacy in 1967 of Eugene McCarthy, because they did not operate in a frame of reference that we were familiar with. We look to the leadership of the country for a frame of reference. And when that leadership does not meet our specifications, we fall apart and thereby impede and hurt that leadership.

So the government has a very strong role to play in the way we in the press behave. The press is not an independent entity, making up its mind about something and then proceeding. It's a reactive group without an independent theology or ideology. I think that's often lost sight of in the criticisms of the press.

DWIGHT TEETER: It seems to me that most of the speakers keep saying that the First Amendment is in pretty good shape and that as long as the press is vigorous, we're going to be all right, and the First Amendment will endure. Yet I hear Daniel Schorr saying that the First Amendment is in trouble. I would like to get some recapitulation on this.

My own personal view is that the First Amendment has always been in trouble, and I think that's the nature of the situation. Things wax and wane, but we can't ever say that any freedom is won once and for all.

I remember blithely teaching students that prior restraint was dead in this country. And then along came the Pentagon Papers case.

MARK McKINNON: I'm somewhat bothered by our tendency to keep referring back to the framers' idea of what the First Amendment was supposed to mean. I think by tracing the history of the First Amendment, we can see that it evolved and that what we're worried about now is not its change from what the framers had in mind, but the fact that its growth has been stunted and perhaps even has regressed. So I think when we look at it, we have to think about it in terms of today's society and what differences there are between today and then, and how government is involved in all the elements of our society.

HERBERT SCHMERTZ: To some extent, the First Amendment is in trouble with certain people because of the way newspapers and television have interpreted the privilege that the First Amendment has given us. I cite one particular aspect of it, and that is the application of First Amendment rights to journalists in relation to public figures.

It is clear to many of us that the courts have given to newspaper and television reporters First Amendment privileges that substantially reduce the civil rights of public figures as compared to the average citizen. It's hard for me to understand, under our Constitution, why one group of individuals in our society should have fewer civil rights than any other group. And "public figure" by legal definition goes well beyond the elected public official. It covers almost anybody who's in the news.

The *Times* editorialized about this recently in relation to the *National Enquirer* case. But look at *New York Times* v. *Sullivan*,* and the burden of proof of malice, or the proof of reckless disregard for the facts, and the fact that newspapers won't divulge sources—even proving malice is an impossible burden, and it puts public figures in a substantially less advantageous position than that of the average citizen. That, in part, is why you're hearing complaints about the First Amendment.

DANIEL SCHORR: I will tell you why I think the First Amendment is in trouble, and I will try to go easy on the legal side of it, especially since there are a great many wiser legal heads than mine. It is fairly clear, however, that in the past few years—from the *Branzburg* case† in regard to sources, to the *Stanford* case ‡ in regard to newsroom searches, to the *Boston Bank* case, § in which Chief Justice Burger delivered some totally gratuitous remarks

---

*In 1964, the Supreme Court broadened the protection of the mass media against defamation judgments in *New York Times Co.* v. *Sullivan* (376 U.S. 265, 84 S. Ct. 710 [1964]). In that case, a libel action had been brought by the Montgomery, Alabama, police chief following *Times* reports of mishandling of civil rights demonstrations in Montgomery. The Supreme Court absolved the newspaper, ruling that a public official must demonstrate that information was published "with knowledge that it was false or with reckless disregard of whether it was false or not." The Court said that a "profound national commitment to the principle that debate on public issues should be uninhibited, robust, and wide-open" prevents recovery for libel in reports about the public acts of public officials unless actual malice is present.

†See note on the *Branzburg* decision on page 62.

‡The Supreme Court upheld court-approved searches of newspaper offices by police in a 5-3 decision, May 31, 1978. In *Zurcher* v. *Standford Daily* (436 U.S. 547, 98 S. Ct. 1970 [1978]), the Court held that a person not involved in a crime has no more right than a suspect to resist a search of a building he owns or occupies for evidence of someone else's crime. The ruling reversed decisions by two lower courts in the case involving a search of the offices of the Stanford campus newspaper in 1971. Police officers entered the newspaper office armed with a warrant authorizing them to search for photographic evidence concerning a clash between police and demonstrators. The *Daily* brought a civil action charging violations of the First, Fourth, and Fourteenth amendments. The *Daily* won its case in the lower courts, but the police appealed the decision. Justice Byron R. White said, "Surely a warrant to search newspaper premises for criminal evidence...for news photographs taken in a public place carries no realistic threat of prior restraint or of any direct restraint whatsoever on the publication of the *Daily* or on its communication of ideas."

§On April 26, 1978, the Supreme Court struck down 5-4 a Massachusetts law restricting political spending by corporations (*First National Bank of Boston et al.* v. *Francis X. Bellotti* [435 U.S. 765, 98 S. Ct. 1407 (1978)]). In a concurring opinion, Chief

about the "imperial press" and the "imperial news media"—the courts in general have begun to curb the operation of the First Amendment, at least in terms of privilege as we would like to have it.

Earlier there were remarks—all too flippant remarks I'm afraid—about the media's asking for special privileges that did not belong to others. The fact that one has to make a case on the other side in this company is an indication of how far First Amendment privilege has slipped.

This society will grant a special privilege when it is considered to be a social good. It will relieve a lawyer from having to testify about what a client has said. It will relieve, in most cases, a doctor from having to testify about what a patient said. It will relieve a priest from having to testify about what is said during a confession.

These are special privileges, special privileges that no one questions because they are considered to be important to the operation of our society.

Journalists tried to say, and did say in the case of *Branzburg v. Caldwell*,* that there is a bridge between the press and the people. The press serves a special function outside the normal operation of government. If you want to know what's going on that's wrong, we can find out for you in ways which prosecutors cannot. We will go and talk to people. We can't use their names because they may go to jail for that, but we will give you some idea of what Black Panthers think and what they do and why they do it.

If you accept that as social good, then you say, "Well,

Justice Warren Burger raised some questions he said were "likely to arise in this area in the future." He wrote at some length about "media conglomerates," saying, "Making traditional use of the corporate form, some media enterprises have amassed vast wealth and power and conduct many activities, some directly related—and some not—to their publishing and broadcasting activities." Burger said that such media conglomerates could pose "a much more realistic threat" to "valid interests" in the electoral process than corporations not regularly concerned with shaping popular opinion on public issues. He concluded by stating that "the First Amendment does not 'belong' to any definable category of persons or entities; it belongs to all who exercise its freedoms."

*The *Caldwell* case was part of what is collectively referred to as the *Branzburg* decision of the Supreme Court (See note on page 62.) Earl Caldwell, a *New York Times* reporter in San Francisco, had covered Black Panther activities and was called to testify before a federal grand jury. He refused to appear and the lower courts ruled that a qualified privilege exists for newspeople and that it applied to Caldwell. However, the Supreme Court ruled that the newsperson's obligation is to respond to grand jury subpoenas as other citizens do, and to answer questions relevent to criminal proceedings.

obviously you have to keep your sources confidential because without being able to promise confidentiality, you wouldn't have had the story in the first place and people wouldn't know what was going on."

My own father went to jail for breaking a story, and if he hadn't broken the story there wouldn't have been any case at all, because his investigation caused it and he needed his notes and his sources to be able to follow through. If society accepts that, then that is reflected in the courts. Society no longer accepts that, and why does society no longer accept that? Because the image of Hildy Johnson from *The Front Page*,* poor, drunk, and with a press card in his greasy hatband, fighting city hall, is no longer true; because there have been cases such as when NBC claimed protection of the First Amendment for its right—and it surely is there—to make a production about rape, even if that rape is then imitated by somebody. And *Hustler* magazine goes in and asks the protection of the First Amendment for something close to pornography.

The amendment has been stretched in such a way—not by poor young reporters—but by a giant industry to protect what inevitably becomes profit-making and not just an attempt to keep people informed. And as a result, there were no picket lines outside the courtroom when my own father went to jail, although you can get a picket line on any abortion issue you want.

That is what I mean when I say the First Amendment is in trouble. You cannot go to an ordinary group of Americans and get them to understand that the First Amendment does not merely serve those of us in the press—it is also meant to serve them. They once did accept that; they don't any longer because it has been covering too many other things.

FROM THE AUDIENCE: Members of the panel have touched on issues concerning responsibility and irresponsibility of the press. I would like to return for a moment to something that Mr. Day said earlier concerning the Bay of Pigs.

**The Front Page, a play written by Ben Hecht and Charles MacArthur, is a portrayal of newspaper life. The comedy-drama, first produced in 1928, is set in Chicago and features the more flamboyant and racy aspects of popular journalism of the day. Hildy Johnson was the central character, described by the playwrights as "a vanishing type—the lusty, hoodlumesque, half-drunken caballero that was the newspaperman of our youth." A movie version of *The Front Page* was made in 1931.

When does a conflict arise between the press's dual responsibilities to report the news to the American public and also to protect the welfare of people, perhaps soldiers, involved in such a secret operation? Don't those two responsibilities, both to report the news and to be a responsible member of our society, conflict and form a sort of paradox which can only result in irresponsibility? How does the press resolve that kind of conflict?

ANTHONY DAY: That's a very good question. It's a very difficult one. The answer, which sounds terribly arrogant but isn't actually, is that in the end, the editors and the reporters are the ones who decide that. The governments generally make extravagant claims for national security— extravagant overclaims for national security.

The closest case recently came in the publication of some data involving the particular American scheme for making the hydrogen bomb, and the press was quite divided over whether that little piece of information, that little diagram, should have been published. As it turned out, it already had been published by the government and declassified by the government.* So the whole great argument just collapsed.

In general, I think you'll find that in matters like kidnappings or technical CIA operations—spy satellites and that sort of thing—the press is pretty good, deciding that it's in its own interest and the people's interest to keep that sort of technical detail secret.

I think generally, though, when it comes to large decisions about information that may affect the people of the United States, the movement in the last several years has been toward revealing it, in one way or another.

HERBERT SCHMERTZ: Could I just make a comment on that? First of all, I don't think it's the journalists who make the decision. I think it's the courts which make the decision.

Secondly, I don't think journalists are competent to make decisions as to whether you will or will not declassify information. That's not your job. It is the government's job to decide whether it is going to declassify. If you disagree with me, you take it to court.

ANTHONY DAY: We publish tons of declassified information every single day, as everybody here who has worked for the government knows.

---

*This refers to the *Progressive* magazine controversy. (See note on page 39.)

HERBERT SCHMERTZ: I'm not very secure in delegating to the press the responsibility to declassify security information.

JODY POWELL: You might expect that I'm not either.

I would like to make one other point. You cannot say on the one hand, "We take unto ourselves the right to make this decision and unto ourselves alone," and say on the other to me as a spokesman for the government, "I expect you not to lie to me."

ANTHONY DAY: I didn't say that to you, Jody.

JODY POWELL: I know, nor did anybody else say that I should not lie to you.

I think you start down a path there when you claim too much for yourselves and too much authority in an area in which you also have to accept the consequences in terms of other people's behavior.

ANTHONY DAY: Take the hydrogen bomb case. Now, in our particular case, my newspaper argued against publishing the information on the hydrogen bomb case, and there was much attack by some of our colleagues. But anyway, take that case. Suppose six newspapers have this information and no order has been issued. They're the ones who are going to have to decide whether to publish or not. Some tried and some didn't. In the end, some published and some didn't.

That is the real world. It comes down to the newspapers' judgment.

DANIEL SCHORR: May I suggest the issue has been imprecisely put and is resulting in some confusion?

Newspapers, news media, reporters, and editors do not classify or declassify information. There exists in the government the power to classify information. There exists also in the government the power to hold onto its classified information, and it should make every effort to do so. And when, as in the incident that was cited earlier, an important intelligence source—namely, the ability to monitor what was being said in Brezhnev's car—is leaked, it is unfortunate. That was a very serious violation of security by somebody who was entrusted with the security of that information and, if he could have been found, he should have been punished. But once that information is out, it is not classified information anymore. It's out.

There is a barrier between the government and the free press, and if you can keep information inside your barrier—

and as a citizen, I hope in many cases you do, but not as often as you would like to—then it's your job and your responsibility to do it. But if that horse has left that stable, you can no longer chase it by injunction or by any other way.

There is a bill now winding its way through Congress that would in fact try to do that with names of intelligence agents; it would forbid their publication even if the information were derived from public sources, for example, which is typically how you get names of intelligence agents—by studying the foreign service register.

But the fact of the matter is that the issue has never been clearly drawn. The journalist, or his editor, on rare occasions can be appealed to—as happened successfully with the *New York Times* in the case of the Bay of Pigs and as happened again successfully with the *Washington Post* in the case of the Cuban missile crisis. They can be appealed to to withhold certain information, or to withhold it for a time, or to modify certain parts of it in the public and national interest. In most cases, newspapers and broadcasters will do that.

But to speak of information as though an editor classifies or declassifies, or to raise the idea of going to a judge who knows less about it than either the original classifying authority or the editor and make it an issue of court—which implies an issue of prior restraint—puts us all on the wrong track. To start with, the government should keep classified information classified.

HERBERT SCHMERTZ: But, if a piece of classified information is stolen from the government and given to a newspaper, it seems to me the government has the right to retrieve that stolen property. I know of cases of stolen documents that have gone to the Supreme Court.

DWIGHT TEETER: Obviously, this was a very good question. And if an immoderate moderator might throw in his two cents worth, I'm still wondering why the Army classified the crossbow in the 1960s as top secret, but I'll pass beyond that.

FROM THE AUDIENCE: We have been talking all day about "the press" as if print media and electronic media are all the same, and yet it seems to have been suggested that the electronic news media is more show-business oriented. If this is true, can we continue to put them both under one umbrella? Can we talk about "the press" as including both?

PETER BRAESTRUP: I may have indicated my deep bias in favor of the Gutenberg boys, as they are called by some of my friends in TV. I think there is a real difference between print and television, both in their relationship to the federal government—television is a regulated industry to some degree—and in their internal incentives. There is in the field a very remarkable segregation, whether you're in Vietnam or in Washington, between the print and television. They operate differently. Everybody here has made that clear.

Now, the TV people want to be wrapped in the same First Amendment flag as the print boys.

DANIEL SCHORR: A person can dream.

PETER BRAESTRUP: So far, there has been a certain sense of social insecurity among television people because the print people don't quite regard them as acceptable. So it's a kind of social thing.

DANIEL SCHORR: Oh, boy. The next time we're asked to get on a panel show, we'll get into that.

PETER BRAESTRUP: I understand. I understand.

But to be serious one minute, I think it would be very dangerous for the law, in terms of the First Amendment—that is, in terms of various protections now afforded them both, not privileges but current basic protections—for there to be much differentiation.

I have one last point to make, which is a factual research question.

Research shows that there is a different audience for the two media, too. The evening news shows that attract thirty million people on a given night do not have many loyal followers. Surveys have been done by Professor Larry Lichty of the University of Maryland. He has examined this, and he found that of the 78 million television households in the country, only half watch TV evening news shows as often as once a month. Of those households that do watch TV news at all during the month, only 6 percent watch as often as four nights a week. So the public must sense a difference, too.

HODDING CARTER: I want to add something to this.

On the question of extension of the basic rights of press across the board—and that's a recurring debate—it's interesting to note that the argument in favor of a more restrictive view of press freedom for the broadcast medium derives from the notion of scarcity of a commodity provided by the government to a special vendor. The funny thing is that in 1981 America, scarcity has not been the name of the game in the electronic field. It's the name of the game in the print field. It might really be time now, with the explosion of cable, with the fact that you have—how many?—eight thousand, twelve thousand radio stations and you have more TV stations now than you'll ever have newspapers, to rethink even that barrier which exists in the way both are treated when it comes to First Amendment privileges, rights, and coverage. The law that basically governs broadcasts today no longer has anything to say to the current reality as opposed to the reality at the time at which it was written in the thirties.

FROM THE AUDIENCE: This is for Herbert Schmertz.

I don't have $250,000 to spend responding to an editorial comment that Mobil Corporation or Mobil Oil might make on a commercial network. Do you not think it is irresponsible for CBS to sell its highly impressionable products to the highest bidders to spread their commercial or, I should say, political rhetoric and propaganda?

HERBERT SCHMERTZ: Well, CBS has all kinds of resources to give you an opportunity to respond. They have talk shows. They have interview shows. They provide an abundance of opportunities. And indeed, our perception of what is seen on the network is that the vast amount of free time is being used to present views that are contrary to ours. We were really trying to correct that imbalance to some extent by buying a small amount of paid time. So I don't think you would be disadvantaged if you had something you wanted to say, and indeed, CBS has the resources to correct that imbalance.

FROM THE AUDIENCE: This is a two-part question.

In the hours after the assassination attempt on President Reagan, all three networks reported that Press Secretary James Brady was dead. CBS News went so far as to say he was dead. Dan Rather gave a moment of silence for James Brady.

I would like the panel to comment on that, and also I would like the panel to comment on the fact that the State Department doesn't want to extend Arbatov's* visa so he may appear on television to debate with three Soviets and three Americans.

---

*Dr. Georgi A. Arbatov, Director of the Institute of the United States and Canadian Studies of the Soviet Union. (See note on page 34.)

DANIEL SCHORR: Can I take the first half of that? Would it surprise you to know that the incorrect information about the death of Jim Brady came from the White House and was given to the Senate Majority and Minority leaders and the House Speaker and the House Minority Leader and that it leaked out from there? The reason the networks were so sure of it was that they were told that it came from the White House. No one is quite clear yet about how that happened.

But the larger question you raise is really a very tough question. I was talking earlier about manipulation. There was every evidence that on the day of that shooting, the White House was being very careful to manipulate the way that story was played. It appears to be true that they did not know immediately that the President had been hit. When they said he hadn't been hit, that was an honest mistake.

On the other hand, they knew that within a few seconds of getting in his car, he was coughing up blood and that he staggered into the hospital and almost collapsed. In spite of this, they gave out stories about his going into the hospital under his own power, reeling off funny one-liners.

They also denied there had been any problem between General Haig, Secretary of State, when he came out and made a statement, and Defense Secretary Weinberger, when, in fact, there was a problem, a very important problem. General Haig had given his assurance, trying to reassure everybody, that there was no special military alert ordered, when Secretary Weinberger had just ordered an increased readiness of troops around the world. And later on when they discussed it, Haig asked him to call off that alert and Weinberger reminded him, in case he had forgotten, that the national command authority goes from the President or Vice-President to the Secretary of Defense and not to the Secretary of State, even if he is a retired four-star general.

What I'm saying is that between the unavoidable confusion and the signs of deliberate manipulation of public opinion that went on that day, it is understandable that when a statement is made—based on what you think comes from a good source—you will go with it and it may be a mistake. It is regrettable and unfortunate and would be less likely to happen—and I'm sorry if I take this parochial view of it—if you thought the White House was leveling with you from beginning to end.

HODDING CARTER: Oh, Dan, that's nonsense. Come on.
The imperatives of your business are going to guarantee that it's going to happen again and again. "You can put it in the bank, Walter" was first said not about Jim Brady being dead, but about Mr. Ford's becoming the vice-presidential nominee at the Republican convention. "You can bank on it, Walter."

It is a necessity to be definitive when you don't even have half the facts. It is a continuing problem of television journalism.

DANIEL SCHORR: That was a rumor started by Ford.

HODDING CARTER: I don't care who it was started by. The one thing you don't have to do is to pose as the pundit who knows. Why not be what we all are, reporters who have a barely tangible grasp on reality, and present it that way?

ANTHONY DAY: Dan, I think, too, it's unfair to say for sure that the White House was trying to manipulate the news of the President's condition, because that came out in pretty complicated ways. And it's not at all clear to me, and certainly to our reporters in Washington, that it was deliberate. It may have been accidental. In fact, the President was, for a man who had been shot as it turned out, in very good shape indeed. He did walk into the hospital. He did make one-liners, he did talk, and he did joke. So there is really no evidence that they deliberately tried to make him appear better than he actually was.

DANIEL SCHORR: The White House asked the medical staff to be very careful about what they said. And at eight o'clock in the evening with Dr. O'Leary* was giving his briefing, by then with the President out of danger, he still did not mention that the President had come into the hospital coughing up blood, near shock, and on the point of collapse, at a time when he knew the whole picture. That was still left out, and later he had to have another briefing to catch up with some of those details.

ANTHONY DAY: They are details. The President had been shot. I presumed he was coughing up blood. He had been shot in the lung, for heaven's sake.

JODY POWELL: Let me say one other thing here. My daddy used to accuse me, when I was a kid, of walking around in the back yard with absolutely nobody else there or within

---

*Dr. Dennis O'Leary, Dean of Clinical Affairs at George Washington University Hospital, briefed the press on President Reagan's condition following the attempted assassination of the President.

sight and stubbing my toe on a big oak root and then standing there and screaming in rage, "Look what you made me do."

It seems to me that when you folks get something wrong, it not only was honest and innocent but it wasn't even your fault. If a press spokesman comes out and makes a mistake, the whole thing is turned around.

It has to be some attempt to be manipulative, to deceive the public. There must be back there some deep and dark selfish end to it. I mean, my word, any White House operation that did not, at that hospital, at the very least ask the medical staff to be very careful about what they said about the health of the President of the United States would have been absolutely remiss in their responsibility. It's a pity that somebody didn't make that same request of some other folks who were involved in it.

DWIGHT TEETER: What we have had here is, I think, pretty much what I think of as the responsibility of the news media, the responsibility of citizens. It is to freely search for the truth. We're not always going to find it, and you can see that some of us don't even always agree on what should be some pretty elemental fact situations.

Concluding Remarks by JIM LEHRER

First, before all of you as my witness, I would like to say that I am leaving television journalism. I no longer want to taint myself, and I'm going to return to the *Dallas Times-Herald* and the *Dallas Morning News*, the printed press, the great printed press, the great, great printed press, to that great area where only the real journalists live and work and inform all of us what we need to know.

Listening to this discussion, it occurred to me there are two things I wouldn't want to be. Number one is a TV man. Number two is the last speaker on the program.

Another thing occurred to me, watching—with great amusement on my part—Jody Powell and Herb Schmertz sitting next to each other. When it was announced that Mr. Schmertz was taking a leave of absence to go from Mobil Oil to handle public relations for the Ted Kennedy campaign, Jody Powell was asked at a White House press briefing the next day, "What do you think about that?" Mr. Powell said, "I just hope Mr. Schmertz is as successful in enhancing the public image of Ted Kennedy as he has been of the oil industry in this country."

There is an advantage to being the last speaker and a whole potful of disadvantages. The advantage is simply that this is it. You can't lay a hand on me once I have spoken. The disadvantages are obvious. Twenty people have spoken, and for anybody, much less a TV type, to try to summarize in a very few minutes what these people have had to say and to do their ideas and their thoughts justice would be absurd.

All of you have your impressions of John Connally's desire for more good news; of Harrison Salisbury's answer: "Well, go to Russia, Big John, if that's what you want"; of Joe Kraft's surprising confession that both the front and the back of his mind are identical; of the sayings of Thomas Gibbs Gee: "I can't describe it, but I'd know it if I saw it," and "Where the rubber meets the road." I've never heard that last one before and I'm from Texas.

And we're all going to have our impressions of Jody Powell's not-too-subtle point. Did you listen carefully to what he said right at the beginning? Here's what he said: If the press of this nation had been more diligent and had done a better job of informing the American people of the issues that confronted them before November, he wouldn't have been here today.

Frankly, I think it's fantastic that we of the press got beat up on all day. We deserve it, not necessarily for some of the reasons cited by the attackers, although in some cases I think they were right on target.

I think our major problem, our real problem is that somehow we have gotten it into our heads that we are truly the special people of this world, because we happened into journalism. In my case, it was because I was too small to play sports, and I got interested in sports writing, and here I am, suddenly interviewing people about great issues of our time. But the fact that we went into journalism somehow gave us a special privilege and we became privileged people, above all laws, above all rules that the rest of society have to play by, and they have to damn well play by them because if they don't, we in the press will cut their heads off and print it or put it on the air.

It's a double standard I, for one, can no longer defend and I'm delighted to see that many of the panelists today from the same line of work can't either. It's a double standard that says the courts are right when they order a President of the United States to surrender tapes of his most intimate conversations in the Oval Office but wrong when they order a reporter to turn over notes that could bear on whether a person goes to prison or to the electric chair; a double standard that says it's wrong for a member of Congress to own a piece of an oil well and also vote on energy legislation but right for a newspaper publisher or a newspaper columnist to own stock in an oil company and editorially support the deregulation of crude oil prices; a double standard that allows a national TV reporter to accuse a politician of not addressing the real issues in a report about how that politician stumbled over a word in a speech; a double standard that permits a TV newscaster to read his ad lib happy-talk lines to the weatherman off a teleprompter in the same newscast with a story lamenting the fact that some politician read a one-liner off an index card; a double standard that says it's all right for a newspaper to lead the paper with leak stories about Abscam while on the editorial page in the same edition it condemns the leakers—not the newspaper but the leakers—for unfairly impugning the reputation of Congress; a double standard that, frankly, finally, and generally, says everybody is fair game to society's criticisms and restraints except us—us, the perfect ones of the press.

I am not perfect. Like Peter Braestrup, I have made mistakes in my twenty years in newspaper and TV journalism. Some have been mistakes in judgment, others mistakes in reporting and editing. I have left things in that should have been left out. I have taken things out that should have stayed in. I have misunderstood what somebody told me, and thus distorted that person's real meaning.

I have gotten carried away with a certain story and thus gone too far. I have at times been sloppy in my reporting, overwrought in my writing, careless in my editing. In short, just about every mistake it's possible to make in my line of work I have indeed made. And I am certain that I will make many more before I finally hang it up. I am just as certain that there is not a journalist in this room who wouldn't have to make the same confession.

My point is, let's knock off the "perfect" bit. Okay? We are not perfect, so who in the world do we think we're fooling? We're certainly not fooling the people we're supposedly doing it all for—our readers, our viewers, our listeners. They're on to us and they're on to us in a big way.

I'm more concerned about that, frankly, than I am about what all the John Connallys and the Jody Powells and the other people in government would say about the press. It's the public that we're supposed to be serving and what they think about us really does bother me.

They have become very sophisticated in their so-called media watching. They recognize bad reporting and bad editing when they see it. They know what John Connally knows, too, that the people who work as journalists in this country are not superhumans. They know journalists get tired and they get pushed by deadlines and they blow it just like they do in their own jobs. That's the reason our pious posturings of perfection do not wash with people and never will. And that's the reason when we scream, as we should, about the latest First Amendment outrage, they tune us out, because we've gotten ourselves in a very awkward predicament.

Here we are, claiming to be the servants only of the public interest, claiming we do our thing only because the public has the right to know, claiming it's not us who get hurt by infringements on the freedom of the press, but the people. We scream and we holler all of this, and what do the people say? Usually, they say nothing or, worse than that, they say, "Well, it's about time you arrogant dips in the press got yours."

When we have to tell them that we're their servants, that "it's all for you we're doing it," then something is drastically wrong. In that respect, Dan Schorr is right when he says the First Amendment has got some problems. Frankly, I believe it's our own fault and it's our own job to do something about it. And screaming and hollering about the First Amendment isn't the place to begin; it's the place to end.

We have to go back to the real beginning with the public. We have to do a lot of explaining. We have, first of all, to explain exactly what journalism is. It's not history. There are a lot of people who would like to make it history and who would like to act like it's history, but it isn't history. It's only what happened on a given day or a given group of days. We have to explain that all of us in it or at least most of us in it are trying very, very hard to get it right, but sometimes we get it wrong because of deadline pressures, because of simple human failings, because of reasons beyond our control.

We need to explain that there are indeed legitimate reasons why a reporter, as a matter of routine course, must use confidential sources, reasons that really do affect their rights, the public's rights, a lot more than they affect the individual reporter's. We have to explain that ten thousand cars driven safely on Interstate 35 from Austin to Fort Worth is not news. A three-car accident among the 10,001, '2, and '3, is news. We have to explain that when two newspapers or two television or radio newscasts—despite what John Connally says—do lead with the same story on any given day, it is not necessarily the result of a conspiracy, but it's usually the result of news judgments that occasionally happen to coincide.

We have to explain that journalism is populated by individualists who by and large are disorganized, unorganizable, and the least likely members of society to be involved in any conspiracy, an evil one or a good one, on behalf of John Connally and his folks.

We have to explain that journalists are motivated by many of the same kinds of things that motivate everybody else who works for a living—simply ambition, pride, avarice, greed, etc. And we have to explain that the percentage of incompetents and reprobates is no higher or lower among journalists than it is in any other segment of the population.

In other words, if we want the public to understand what we're doing for them, then we have to bring them under the tent. We have to play it straight and open with them, tell them what we're doing, why we're doing it. We have to stop defending the indefensible. We have to acknowledge our mistakes and correct them as best we can. We have to clean up our own ethics. We have to eliminate every smell of double standard. We have to expose ourselves to the same kind of public scrutiny that we demand of every other segment of public life.

We do not need to prove to our readers and our listeners that we deserve their trust. We have to prove it every day. Then and only then will they respond to our calls in relationship to the First Amendment and respond to the unwarranted criticism of the press that comes from others.

That's not going to happen, in my opinion, until we all take a vow of humility, until we acknowledge privately and publicly that we are not the special people of the world—only our work is. It is convincing people of that specialness that I believe is the mission for all of us who are in journalism, all of us who care about journalism.

To quote from a speech to a recent journalism gathering by Anthony Lewis of the *New York Times*, "The fault, dear Brutus, is not in the stars but in ourselves." Lewis was quoting, of course, from Shakespeare's *Julius Caesar*.

KF 4774 .A75 P73 1982

DATE DUE			